Challenging Common Core Language Arts Lessons

ADVANCED CURRICULUM FROM THE CENTER FOR GIFTED EDUCATION AT WILLIAM & MARY

Challenging Common Core Language Arts Lessons

Activities and Extensions for Gifted and Advanced Learners in GRADE 3

MOLLY BRYAN TALBOT

William & Mary
School of Education
CENTER FOR GIFTED EDUCATION

P.O. Box 8795
Williamsburg, VA 23187

Edited by Katy McDowall

Cover design by Raquel Trevino and layout design by Allegra Denbo

ISBN-13: 978-1-61821-548-2

Prufrock Press Inc.
P.O. Box 8813
Waco, TX 76714-8813
Phone: (800) 998-2208
Fax: (800) 240-0333
http://www.prufrock.com

TABLE OF CONTENTS

INTRODUCTION 1

Unit I: Choices

Lesson 1.1: What Do You Think While Reading? 9
Lesson 1.2: Characters Make Choices Too 15
Lesson 1.3: Learn About Lincoln 23
Lesson 1.4: Central Choices 31
Unit I: Culminating Essay Prompt 37

Unit II: Culture

Lesson 2.1: Cultural Traditions? 41
Lesson 2.2: Are We All the Same? 49
Lesson 2.3: What Cultural Traditions Can Tell Us 59
Lesson 2.4: Cultures of the Past 65
Lesson 2.5: Can Cultures Change a Person? 71
Unit II: Culminating Essay Prompt 75

Unit III: Beliefs

Lesson 3.1: Belief in the Unknown 79
Lesson 3.2: Shoot for the Moon 85
Lesson 3.3: Believe in Yourself 95
Lesson 3.4: People Hold Beliefs 103
Unit III: Culminating Essay Prompt 108

Unit IV: Perseverance

Lesson 4.1: The Importance of Perseverance 111
Lesson 4.2: The Power of Perseverance 117
Lesson 4.3: Perseverance for a Cause 123
Lesson 4.4: Perseverance by Children 127
Lesson 4.5: Flying High With Perseverance 133
Unit IV: Culminating Essay Prompt 140

ANSWER KEY 141

REFERENCES 149

ABOUT THE AUTHOR 151

COMMON CORE STATE STANDARDS ALIGNMENT 153

INTRODUCTION

The Common Core State Standards (CCSS) for English Language Arts (ELA) are K–12 curriculum standards that describe the ELA skills and concepts students need to develop for success in higher education and the 21st-century workplace.

The College and Career Readiness Anchor Standards are the basis of the ELA/literacy standards. They specify the core knowledge and skills needed, while grade-specific standards provide specificity. The ELA standards also establish guidelines for literacy in history/social studies, science, and technical subjects for grades 6–12.

With the adoption of the CCSS in nearly every state, gifted and advanced learners need opportunities to master grade-level standards and ELA skills and concepts with greater depth, rigor, and understanding. This book is one in a series developed in conjunction with the Center for Gifted Education at William & Mary intended to give gifted and advanced learners additional practice and activities to master and engage with the CCSS for ELA. Each book in the series is organized by the content standards in one grade.

The lessons in this book cover grade 3 ELA content. In grade 3, the standards are addressed in five domains:

- Reading Literature and Informational Text,
- Foundational Skills,
- Language,
- Speaking and Listening, and
- Writing.

PURPOSE

The lessons in this book were written with the assumption that a teacher has already introduced ELA content standards through primary curriculum sources. Reading, writing, and speaking activities enrich and extend current grade-level ELA content rather than accelerate students to above-grade-level content. Each lesson focuses on multiple content standards, due to the overlap of skills inherent in ELA activities, and provides additional support and enrichment for gifted and advanced learners.

BOOK AND LESSON STRUCTURE

This book is divided into four units, each of which contains multiple lessons. Each unit focuses on a theme and centers on the ideas related to the theme within literature and nonfiction texts. Within the unit, students will read, analyze, evaluate, and interpret poetry, short stories, and novels containing the theme. Students will demonstrate their growing understanding of this theme through various projects, narrative writing, informational writing, persuasive writing, and presentations.

Each lesson within a unit follows a predictable structure:

- The CCSS that are covered are listed by number.
- Materials, including all student activity pages needed, are also listed. It is assumed students will have access to commonplace items such as pencils and paper, so the materials noted are those that teachers will need to obtain in advance.
- Most required readings (except picture books and read-alouds) are available in Appendix B: Text Exemplars and Sample Performance Tasks of the CCSS ELA document. (See additional information about text selection below.) It is anticipated that using these materials will allow for easy access to appropriate readings. In many cases, the readings that are used may come from the grade-level band above that of the grade level specified for the book.
- The lesson plan includes an estimate for the time it might take to complete the lesson; however, this will vary by teacher and classroom.
- The objectives highlight what students will learn or be able to do as a result of completing the lesson.
- An overview of the lesson's content provides a quick guide to the activities in which the students will be participating.
- A description of prior knowledge needed as a prerequisite for understanding the activities in a lesson is given. The teacher should be sure the students already have a working understanding of this content before beginning the lesson. Because the intended use of the activities is for students who have already mastered the stated standards, the teacher may want to preassess prior to having students complete the activities.
- The instructional sequence provides a detailed description of what the teacher and students will do during the lesson.
- The extension activities listed provide follow-up learning opportunities for students that go beyond the lesson to provide both additional enrichment and extension. Activities may be completed by individuals or groups, and may be completed at school or at home.
- At the end of each unit, a culminating essay is presented to provide closure and to assess students' synthesis of unit ideas.

THE SELECTION OF TEXT EXEMPLARS

The text exemplars selected for the book meet the specific criteria for high-ability learners suggested by Baskin and Harris (1980). These criteria (Center for Gifted Education, 2011) include:

- The language used in texts for the gifted should be rich, varied, precise, complex, and exciting.
- Texts should be chosen with a consideration of their open-endedness and their capacity to inspire thoughtful engagement.
- Texts for the gifted should be complex so that they promote interpretive and evaluative behaviors by readers.
- Texts for the gifted should help them develop problem-solving skills and acquire methods of productive thinking.
- Texts should provide characters as role models.
- Text types should cover a full range of materials and genres. (p. 15)

TOOLS FOR ANALYZING TEXTS

For the majority of the activities in this book, it is recommended that the teacher have students complete the Literature Analysis Model (see Figure 1) as part of their first encounter with the text. When students read the text for the first time, they should annotate it or use text coding (Harvey & Goudvis, 2007) as a metacognitive strategy to aid in comprehension. Once this marking of the text has occurred, the student should use the Literature Analysis Model and engage in a discussion about it (or selected portions) before progressing to other lesson activities.

The Literature Analysis Model encourages students to consider seven aspects of a selection they are reading: key words, tone, mood, imagery, symbolism, key ideas, and the structure of writing (Center for Gifted Education, 2011; McKeague, 2009; National Governors Association Center for Best Practices & Council of Chief State School Officers [NGA & CCSSO], 2010). After reading a selection, this model helps students to organize their initial responses and provides them with a basis for discussing the piece in small or large groups. Whenever possible, students should be allowed to underline and make notes as they read the material. After marking the text, they can organize their notes into the model.

Suggested questions for completing and discussing the model are:

- **Key words:** What words are important for understanding the selection? Which words did the author use for emphasis?
- **Important ideas:** What is the main idea of the selection? What are other important ideas in the selection?
- **Tone:** What is the attitude or what are the feelings of the author toward the subject of the selection? What words does the author use to indicate tone?

HANDOUT

Literature Analysis Model

Chosen or assigned text: ______	
Key words	
Important ideas	
Tone	
Mood	
Imagery	
Symbolism	
Structure of writing	

Figure 1. Literature Analysis Model. *Note.* Adapted from *Exploring America in the 1950s* (p. 10) by M. Sandling & K. L. Chandler, 2014, Waco, TX: Prufrock Press. Copyright 2014 by Center for Gifted Education. Adapted with permission.

- **Mood:** What emotions do you feel when reading the selection? How do the setting, images, objects, and details contribute to the mood?
- **Imagery:** What are examples of the descriptive language that is used to create sensory impressions in the selection?
- **Symbolism:** What symbols are used to represent other things?
- **Structure of writing:** What are some important characteristics of the way this piece is written? How do the parts of this selection fit together and relate to each other? How do structural elements contribute to the meaning of the piece?

After students have completed their Literature Analysis Models individually, they should compare their answers in small groups. These small groups may compile a composite model that includes the ideas of all members. Following the small-group work, teachers have several options for using the models. For instance, they may ask each group to report to the class, they may ask groups to post their composite models, or they may develop a new Literature Analysis Model with the class based on the small-group work. It is important for teachers to hold a whole-group discussion as the final aspect of implementing this model as a teaching-learning device. Teachers are also encouraged to display the selection on a document camera or overhead projector as it is discussed and make appropriate annotations. The teacher should record ideas, underline words listed, and call attention to student responses visually. The teacher should conclude the discussion by asking open-ended follow-up questions. For more information about analyzing literature, see Center for Gifted Education (2011).

GROUPING OPTIONS

The lessons in this book can be used for whole-group, small-group, and individual instruction.

Whole-Group Instruction

Teachers can use this book in one academic year in conjunction with the primary curriculum in a gifted education or advanced ELA class. All students would complete each lesson after being introduced to particular content standards. Teachers can integrate the lessons into the primary curriculum taught to a whole group and address higher order thinking questions through the lesson activities.

Small-Group Instruction

Teachers can use this book to differentiate learning in any ELA class by creating flexible student groups and giving students who need enrichment an opportunity for deeper understanding and engagement with a concept. Students can complete activities and practice at a self-guided pace with a partner or small group and engage in peer discussion, with or without directed supervision or intervention from the teacher.

Individual Instruction

The activities and questions in each lesson are a good way to determine individual understanding of a certain ELA concept on a deeper level.

AUTHOR'S RATIONALE FOR THE TEXTS AND THEMES SELECTED

The selection of texts and accompanying themes explored in this manual were chosen with careful consideration of several factors: quality of fictional literature and informational texts, appropriateness of the texts for developmental age, accessibility of texts for the average teacher, and relatability of themes to third-grade students. The CCSS's list of exemplar texts was also considered in the collection of texts so as to help serve as a purpose for validation for teachers in states that have adopted the standards.

The quality of fictional literature and informational texts is extremely important when choosing texts for gifted and advanced learners. Students need opportunities to explore a variety of high-quality texts in order to further develop advanced reading skills and to foster habits of mind desired in the language arts. One example of such a story is *My Father's Dragon*, which uses wonderful word choice and imagery to bring the story to life. Exposure to high-quality texts in units such as the ones included in this book will also teach readers to judge texts' appropriateness in order to independently select texts throughout their lives.

The texts chosen for this book have messages and characters that are developmentally suitable for students. As advanced readers, gifted students often struggle with finding appropriately challenging texts that also meet their academically advanced ELA needs. Through the higher order reasoning questions, resulting discussions, and student-created products associated with these texts, gifted and advanced students' needs are met while still maintaining messages and characters to which students can relate. Many texts used in the unit are considered "Read Aloud" texts according to Appendix B of the CCSS, such as *Lincoln: A Photobiography*. Texts such as these are more advanced for the average student and therefore need to be read aloud by a teacher; however, an advanced reader should be capable of working with this text independently or with a small group.

Text accessibility was another consideration when choosing texts for this book. The majority of texts used in lessons in the units are available free and online at the time of printing. In addition, the use of Common Core Exemplar Texts for the anchor texts for each lesson will, hopefully, give teachers some power when convincing schools or districts to purchase class sets of the texts. However, the activities and questions could apply to a wide range of similar texts if the teacher is not able to access the suggested anchor texts. Many lessons include such suggested alternate texts; for example, a teacher could easily replace *The Raft* with *A Long Way From Chicago* if desired.

Universal themes are important in the study of literature and nonfiction texts for gifted and advanced students and have thus been implemented as an organizer for the units in this book. Selection of literature and nonfiction must be carefully considered when teaching for conceptual understanding, as must the relatability of themes to the student to which the lessons are directed. Themes such as choices, culture, beliefs, and perseverance are themes that students will be exposed to in the units seen here. Each of these themes was chosen with advanced third-grade students in mind and their emerging need to learn more about themselves, their world, and how to work through adversity to accomplish their goals.

UNIT I

Choices

This unit centers on the theme of choice, as related to choices people, authors, and characters make within literature and nonfiction texts. Within the unit, students will read, analyze, evaluate, and interpret poetry, short stories, and literature with themes related to choices and the effects of those choices. Students will consider choices made by characters, authors, and even themselves as they work to develop a deeper understanding of choice in literature and nonfiction. Students will demonstrate their growing understanding of this theme through various projects, narrative writing, informational writing, and presentations.

LESSON 1.1

What Do You Think While Reading?

Common Core State Standards

- RL.3.1
- RL.3.4
- RL.3.5
- RF.3.4a
- W.3.4
- W.3.5
- W.3.6
- W.3.8
- SL.3.1
- SL.3.4
- SL.3.5
- SL.3.6
- L.3.1
- L.3.3
- L.3.5

Materials

- Lesson 1.1 Literature Analysis Model
- Lesson 1.1 Thinking While Analyzing Poetry
- Lesson 1.1 Rubric: Gary Soto Figurative Language
- Student copies of "Eating While Reading" by Gary Soto
- Computer and Internet access
- Projector to show video clip

Estimated Time

- 120 minutes

Objectives

In this lesson, students will:

- read and analyze a poem to determine literal and nonliteral meanings of words,
- write an original poem in the style of a mentor poem, and
- record a reading of their own poem to demonstrate fluid reading.

Content

Students will analyze a poem by Gary Soto to distinguish literal and nonliteral meanings of words and phrases, understanding why the author chose the words and phrases for the overall effect of the poem. Students will create their own poem in the style of Soto's "Eating While Reading" to use nonliteral language to express what reading means to them. Students will then choose or draw pictures to illustrate their poems. Students will create an audio/visual recording of their poem to demonstrate fluid reading and reading with expression. Students will then write a reflective essay about the choices they made when writing their poem.

Prior Knowledge

Students will need to have prior exposure to types of figurative language, specifically alliteration, onomatopoeia, and personification, and poetry structure. Students will also need to have prior knowledge in the use of imagery by poets to create mood in poetry.

> ***Teacher's Note.*** You may not want to tell students the specific pieces of figurative language found in this poem if students have prior knowledge of identifying figurative language.

INSTRUCTIONAL SEQUENCE

1. Conduct a whole-class reading of "Eating While Reading" by Gary Soto. For an initial analysis, work with students to complete Lesson 1.1 Literature Analysis Model. Consider leaving the imagery box blank, as that will be the focus of this lesson. (See pp. 3–4 for additional information about using the Literature Analysis Model.)
2. As a class, discuss how the author uses figurative language to create images in the minds of readers. Guiding questions may include:
   - What do you see when you hear this poem?
   - What vivid words does the author use to create images in the minds of the reader?
   - What line shows an example of imagery that Gary Soto uses in this poem? (Answers will vary, but may include "the balloon of bubble gum" or "slow slither of snow cone syrup running down your arm.")

3. Have pairs do a close read of the poem, looking for examples of figurative language. Encourage students to annotate the text as they read. Examples of figurative language seen include alliteration ("swig of soda," "slow slither of snow cone syrup"), onomatopoeia ("crack"), and personification ("book yells"). Have students complete Lesson 1.1 Thinking While Analyzing Poetry with their partners.
4. Discuss what students found. Encourage students to support their answers with lines from the poem.
5. Ask: *How do you think Gary Soto feels about reading?* Have students discuss within small groups and then as a whole class. Ask: *How did the author's word choice add to your understanding of the poem?* For example, you may want students to notice the use of "swig of soda" as opposed to a "sip of soda."
6. Have students brainstorm what reading means to them and how reading makes them feel. Have them equate reading to another enjoyable activity, as Gary Soto equates the pleasure of consuming a favorite food with the draw of a good book and how both provide an irresistible attraction. Have students share a few examples. Examples may include "singing while reading," "dancing while reading," and "swinging while reading" (baseball).
7. Have students create a poem in the style of "Eating While Reading" to equate reading to another pleasurable activity, using at least three different types of figurative language and descriptive words to create imagery. Students should draw from the ideas that they have brainstormed, considering what types of figurative language will be most appropriate.

Consider doing an example together as a class, using one of the ideas generated previously. Distribute Lesson 1.1 Rubric: Gary Soto Figurative Language before they begin.

> ***Teacher's Note.*** An Exceeds Expectations column has been added to the rubric to encourage students to push themselves beyond the standard expectations. Very few students may rank in this column.

8. (Optional) Have students edit a peer's writing. Students can add "glows" (remarks on outstanding parts of the writing) and "grows" (remarks on where a student might improve the writing) to a peer's writing.
9. Afterward, show a video of Gary Soto's poem (http://www.watchknowlearn.org/Video.aspx?VideoID=36330&CategoryID=10488). Discuss how the images chosen help add to the poem.
10. Have students create their own video version of their poem, using images either found or created by students. Students may use a public domain picture website, such as https://pixabay.com, to find photos to use in their poem.
11. Allow for a movie day in which students share movie poems with their classmates.
12. Have each student write a reflective essay about the choices he or she made when writing his or her poem. This should be a metacognitive piece in which they reflect on why they chose certain figurative language types to express the images they wanted to portray. Have students share their work. During the class discussion, ask:
    - What types of choices did you have to make while writing the poem?
    - How often did you make a choice, then change your mind and rewrite a section? What caused you to change your mind?
    - Why is an author's choice of figurative language so important in poetry writing?
    - Which types of figurative language were particularly useful for writing your poem? Why?

Extension Activities

Students may:

- choose a character from a novel they are reading and write a poem from that character's perspective that explains how the character feels about reading;
- use a novel that they are reading to serve as inspiration for a poem specifically related to the joy the reader gets from reading this novel, which can serve as an advertisement for the novel at the end of a unit; or
- find other examples of poetry that rely heavily on figurative language and share the poem with their classmates, pointing out the figurative language used and why it is effective.

NAME:________________________ DATE:____________

Choices

LESSON 1.1

Literature Analysis Model

Directions: Complete this Literature Analysis Model about "Eating While Reading" by Gary Soto.

	"Eating While Reading" by Gary Soto
Key Words	
Important Ideas	
Tone	
Mood	
Imagery	
Symbolism	
Structure of Writing	

Note. Adapted from *Exploring America in the 1950s* (p. 10) by M. Sandling & K. L. Chandler, 2014, Waco, TX: Prufrock Press. Copyright 2014 by Center for Gifted Education. Adapted with permission.

NAME:______________________________ DATE:______________

LESSON 1.1

Thinking While Analyzing Poetry

Directions: With your partner, complete a close reading for the language used in Gary Soto's poem "Eating While Reading." Record your thoughts in the chart below.

Example of Figurative Language	Stanza and Line Where Example Is Found	How the Author's Use of This Language Adds Meaning to the Poem

Choices

NAME:______________________________ DATE:______________

LESSON 1.1 RUBRIC

Gary Soto Figurative Language Poem

	Exceeds Expectations 5 points	Proficient 4 points	Developed 3 points	Emerging 2 points	Novice 1 point
Ideas in Poem	Created in the style of Gary Soto's "Eating While Reading" and uses personal details to equate reading to a unique, enjoyable activity.	Created in the style of Gary Soto's "Eating While Reading" and uses personal details to equate reading to an enjoyable activity.	Created in the style of Gary Soto's "Eating While Reading" and equates reading to an enjoyable activity.	Created in the style of Gary Soto's "Eating While Reading" and uses many similar ideas to the mentor poem.	Not created in the style of Gary Soto's "Eating While Reading."
Figurative Language and Imagery	Contains at least four different types of figurative language and creates vivid imagery in the mind of the reader.	Contains at least three different types of figurative language and creates imagery in the mind of the reader.	Contains at least two different types of figurative language and creates imagery in the mind of the reader.	Contains at least two different types of figurative language but does not create imagery in the mind of the reader.	Contains fewer than two different types of figurative language and does not create imagery in the mind of the reader.
Poem Structure	Contains at least three 5-line stanzas.	Contains at least two 4-line stanzas.	Contains at least 8 lines, but the lines may not be divided into stanzas.	Contains two stanzas that are fewer than 4 lines each.	Contains fewer than two stanzas or fewer than a total of 6 lines.
Conventions	Demonstrates superior command of the conventions of the English language, with no errors in grammar, spelling, or usage.	Demonstrates command of the conventions of the English language, with no more than one error in grammar, spelling, or usage.	Demonstrates command of the conventions of the English language, with no more than two errors in grammar, spelling, or usage.	Demonstrates command of the conventions of the English language, with no more than three errors in grammar, spelling, or usage.	Demonstrates novice command of the conventions of the English language, with more than three errors in grammar, spelling, or usage.
					________ / 16

Choices

LESSON 1.2

Characters Make Choices Too

Common Core State Standards

- RL.3.1
- RL.3.9
- RL.3.10
- W.3.4
- W.3.10
- SL.3.1
- SL.3.4
- SL.3.6
- L.3.1
- L.3.2
- L.3.3

Materials

- Lesson 1.2 Literature Analysis Model
- Lesson 1.2 Comparing and Contrasting With Allen Say
- Lesson 1.2 Rubric: Letter to Character
- Student copies of *The Sign Painter* by Allen Say
- Student copies of *Grandfather's Journey* by Allen Say

Estimated Time

- 95 minutes

Objectives

In this lesson, students will:

- read in order to provide a comparison and contrast of the themes of stories written by the same author about the same or similar characters, and
- compose a letter from the point of view of one of Allen Say's characters, using traits, actions, and feelings of the character to explain the motivation behind choices made in the story.

Content

Students will read and analyze two short stories by Allen Say to compare and contrast themes and the author's message. Students will then choose one character from one of the stories and write a letter from that character's point of view to another character explaining a life-changing choice that was made in the story.

Prior Knowledge

Students will need to have analyzed and compared texts and central themes by the same author. Students will need to have had practice writing a formal letter.

INSTRUCTIONAL SEQUENCE

1. Discuss what it means to make choices in life. Get students to share examples of choices they have to make on a daily basis (e.g., what should you wear to a friend's house? What type of drink do you want with your lunch?).
2. Then ask students about more difficult choices they may have had to make in life (e.g., should I save my money for something in the future or spend it now? Should I forgive my friend who hurt my feelings at recess?). Ask and discuss:
   - Why might these types of choices require more thought and consideration?
   - How might these choices make a difference in your life?

3. Explain that students will read two stories by Allen Say in which the characters had to make difficult choices that could make a difference in their lives. For an initial analysis of the stories, work with students to complete Lesson 1.2 Literature Analysis Model (about one or both stories) after they have done an initial close reading of the stories. Consider emphasizing specific boxes that will be the focus of this lesson. (See pp. 3–4 for additional information about using the Literature Analysis Model.)
4. Have students work with partners to reread *The Sign Painter* and *Grandfather's Journey*. Before they begin, distribute Lesson 1.2 Comparing and Contrasting With Allen Say. Explain that they will complete the chart and accompanying questions with their partner after rereading the texts. Emphasize that they need to read for enjoyment first, then work on the questions after the text has been read.

Teacher's Note. Depending on time and readiness of students, you may decide to do one story with the question set on one day and the other story with the question set on the following day. You would then follow with the small-group discussions on the next day, as these are both complex texts.

5. Once pairs complete the chart and questions, have them partner with another pair of students to discuss their findings. Afterward, conduct a culminating discussion with the whole group. Guiding questions may include:
   - How does an individual's character traits influence the choices he or she makes?
   - Provide examples of your character traits and how they have influenced your choices.
   - How can having choices be both positive and negative for a person? Give an example from your personal experiences.
   - Reflect about your own life and describe either the best choice you ever made, or the worst one. What was the end result?
   - Think about what you are learning in social studies. Give an example of a choice made by an individual who influenced the course of history.

6. Afterward, ask students to choose one character from either story from whose point of view they will write a letter explaining the reasons for their life-changing choice. The letter

may be addressed to another character in the story or to the teacher. Before students begin, distribute and review Lesson 1.2 Rubric: Letter to Character.

Extension Activities

Students may:

- rewrite the ending of one of the stories focused on the character making a choice different from one that was made in the story, or
- write a sequel to one of the texts using the style of Allen Say as found in *The Sign Painter* or *Grandfather's Journey*.

NAME:______________________________ DATE:______________

Choices

LESSON 1.2

Literature Analysis Model

Directions: Complete the Literature Analysis Model about one or both of the stories written by Allen Say.

	Chosen or Assigned Text: ______________________
Key Words	
Important Ideas	
Tone	
Mood	
Imagery	
Symbolism	
Structure of Writing	

Note. Adapted from *Exploring America in the 1950s* (p. 10) by M. Sandling & K. L. Chandler, 2014, Waco, TX: Prufrock Press. Copyright 2014 by Center for Gifted Education. Adapted with permission.

NAME:______________________________ DATE:______________

LESSON 1.2

Comparing and Contrasting With Allen Say

Directions: Complete the following chart using textual evidence from both Allen Say stories and then answer the questions below, using the information from the chart.

	The Sign Painter	Page Number	*Grandfather's Journey*	Page Number
Choice Made by Main Character				
Effect of the Choice				
Author's Message				

1. How does Allen Say have similar settings in his two short stories?

2. The characters in the two Allen Say stories have similar and different character traits. Use the Venn diagram below to compare and contrast the character traits for the characters in the stories.

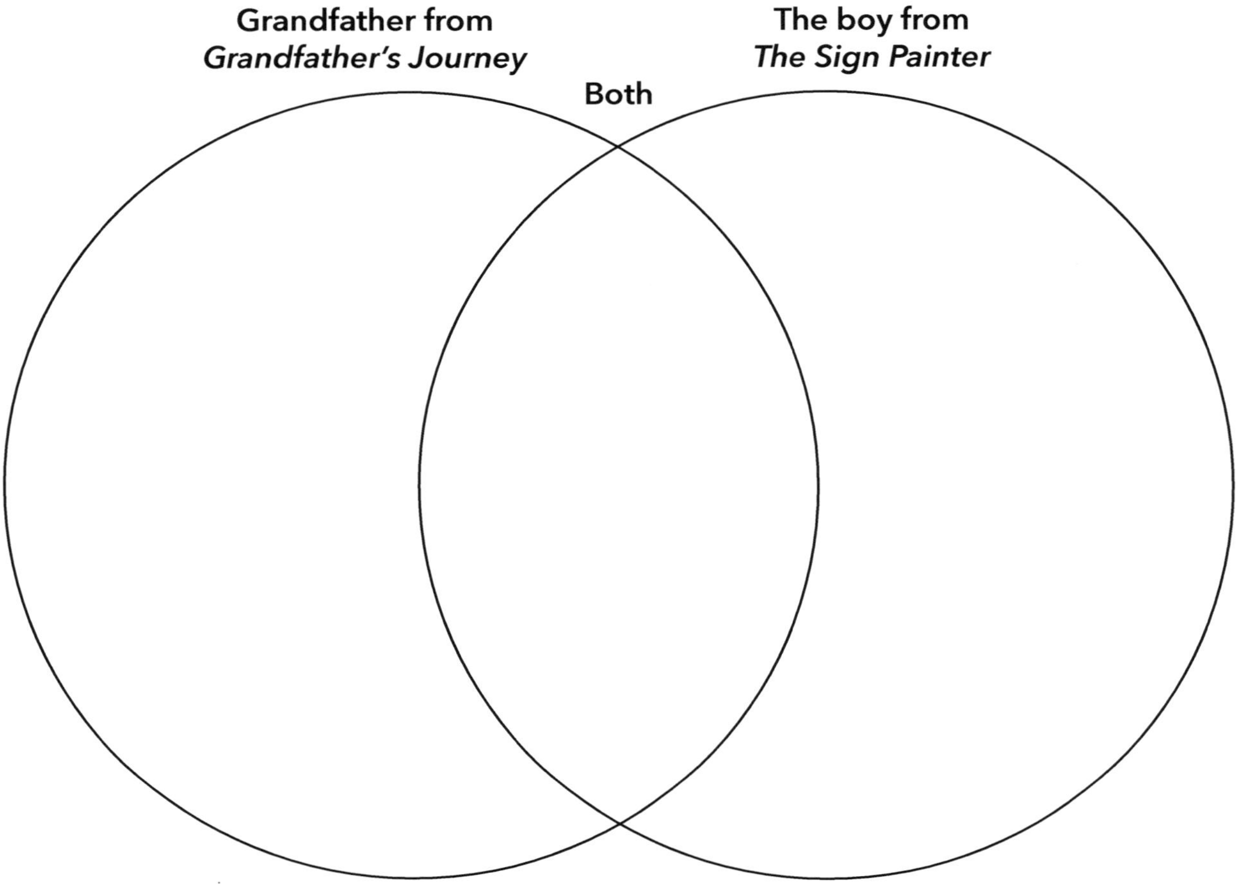

3. How does each character's traits contribute to the choice(s) he made in the story?

4. How are the central messages in both stories similar yet different? How do the characters' choices play a role in developing the central message?

5. Both characters in Allen Say's short stories embark on a journey. Why do you think Allen Say would have his characters make this choice? What traits about each main character would make them suitable for a life of unknown journeys?

NAME:______________________________ DATE:______________

LESSON 1.2 RUBRIC

Letter to Character

	Exceeds Expectations 5 points	Proficient 4 points	Developed 3 points	Emerging 2 points	Novice 1 point
Content	Contains unique details from the story that support reasons as to why an Allen Say character made a choice in the plot of the story.	Contains details from the story that support reasons as to why an Allen Say character made a choice in the plot of the story.	Explains why an Allen Say character made a choice in the plot of the story without using specific details from the story.	Explains why an Allen Say character made a choice in the plot of the story without using any details from the story.	Does not clearly explain why an Allen Say character made a choice in the plot of the story.
Point of View	Clearly written from the character's point of view, as evidenced by specific words, thoughts, and actions the character made in the story.	Clearly written from the character's point of view, as evidenced by specific words, thoughts, or actions the character made in the story.	Written from the character's point of view, with some thoughts, words, or actions the character made in the story.	Written from the character's point of view without specific thoughts, specific thoughts, words, or actions from the text.	Not clear if the letter is written from the character's point of view.
Letter Structure	Has a clear greeting, at least three body paragraphs, a clear closing, and a clear signature.	Has a clear greeting, two body paragraphs, a clear closing, and a clear signature.	Missing one of the following: a clear greeting, two body paragraphs, a clear closing, or a clear signature.	Missing two of the following: a clear greeting, two body paragraphs, a clear closing, or a clear signature.	Missing more than two of the following: a clear greeting, two body paragraphs, a clear closing, or a clear signature.
Conventions	Demonstrates superior command of the conventions of the English language, with no errors in grammar, spelling, or usage.	Demonstrates command of the conventions of the English language, with no more than one error in grammar, spelling, or usage.	Demonstrates command of the conventions of the English language, with no more than two errors in grammar, spelling, or usage.	Demonstrates command of the conventions of the English language, with no more than three errors in grammar, spelling, or usage.	Demonstrates novice command of the conventions of the English language, with more than three errors in grammar, spelling, or usage.
					______ / 16

Choices

LESSON 1.3

Learn About Lincoln

Common Core State Standards

- RI.3.3
- RI.3.5
- RI.3.7
- RI.3.8
- RI.3.9
- RI.3.10
- W.3.7
- W.3.8
- SL.3.1
- SL.3.4
- SL.3.6
- L.3.1
- L.3.2
- L.3.3

Materials

- Lesson 1.3 Exploring Nonfiction Text Features
- Lesson 1.3 Learning About Lincoln
- Lesson 1.3 Research Guide
- Student copies of *Lincoln: A Photobiography* by Russell Freedman
- Computer and Internet access

Estimated Time

- 120 minutes (with additional time set aside for research)

Objectives

In this lesson, students will:

- demonstrate comprehension of nonfiction through answering a series of questions related to the text, and
- complete research on another historical figure to create a photobiography of the historical figure's life.

Content

Students will answer a series of questions after reading a nonfiction text on Abraham Lincoln to show comprehension. Students will choose another historical figure to research and create a short photobiography of the historical figure's life to share through an author's tea with classmates.

Prior Knowledge

Students will need to have read *Lincoln: A Photobiography*. This book is considered a "read-aloud" exemplar text in Appendix B of the CCSS. The Lexile level for this book is 1100, which will be challenging for gifted third graders. Students will need practice using nonfiction text features such as captions, headings, bold print, italics, subtitles, textboxes, table of contents, glossary, and index to find information and answer text-dependent questions. Students may also need to be familiar with how to conduct research using a computer (optional).

Teacher's Note. If you read this text or portions of this text aloud, due to the advanced Lexile level, you should choose portions from Lincoln's early life, the Civil War period, the Gettysburg Address, the post-Civil War period, and Lincoln's end of life.

INSTRUCTIONAL SEQUENCE

1. For the first reading of *Lincoln: A Photobiography*, provide students with Lesson 1.3 Exploring Nonfiction Text Features. Have them complete the handout, paying close attention to the idea that authors make choices about what they do and do not include for specific reasons.
2. Have students create a KWL (know, want to know, learned) chart on what they know about President Lincoln before and during reading the photobiography and what they still want to know about him after reading. Leave the "L" column to be completed after the lesson or after more research on Lincoln (see extension activity). This can be a whole-class activity to hook students or a group or independent activity.
3. Explain to students that they will use the text features they have been learning about to answer text-dependent questions. Distribute Lesson 1.3 Learning About Lincoln. After students complete the handout, discuss the photobiography's text features and how they help the reader learn about Lincoln's life.
4. Explain this problem-based scenario: The publishers of *Lincoln: A Photobiography* liked the format of this book so much, that they are looking for authors to create similar books about other historical figures of the Civil War era or another famous time period. Explain that students will choose a different historical figure to research and learn more about that person's life. Distribute Lesson 1.3 Research Guide and explain that this sheet will help students organize their research notes on their historical figure.
5. Once they have completed their research, they will create a short photobiography of their historical figure's life in the same style as *Lincoln: A Photobiography*. Work with students to determine a rubric for this activity based on what they think is important and should be included in their books.

Teacher's Note. Students may want to include certain text features, such as captions, bold print, titles, subtitles, text boxes, and so forth, but also encourage them to think about content such as early life of the historical figure, major accomplishments of the historical figure, what choices made by the person helped him or her to become a famous historical figure, etc.

6. Allow students time to research and create photobiographies. You may want to include a mini-lesson about the use of photographs in books. Closely examine the photographs of Lincoln in this photobiography and ask:
   - What differences in these photographs do you observe?

- What ideas about Lincoln do the photographs convey to you?
- Why do you think the author chose to use these photographs?

7. Students may want to use resources such as those found at http://gws.ala.org/category/history-biography, as it is a student-friendly site with reliable information. They may also use public domain photographs that can be found online, but review copyright information with students. Explain that students will need to use citations for photographs taken from websites or books that contain copyrighted images. A mini-lesson may be needed to show students how to cite information properly. You may ask students to illustrate their photobiography if technology is not available.
8. Upon completion of the photobiographies, host an author's tea in which students are allowed to set up a table with their photobiographies and display their books to classmates. Consider inviting parents, administrators, or other classes.

Extension Activities

Students may:

- research any "want to know" topics that were not answered by additional research for this lesson, or
- make their own photobiography of their life and the choices they have made thus far.

NAME: ______________________ DATE: ______________

Choices

LESSON 1.3

Exploring Nonfiction Text Features

Directions: Look through your book for each of the features listed in the chart. Mark "yes" or "no" to show whether you saw each item. Write a sentence or two to explain what you could tell about the book from each feature. Some hints and questions are included in the boxes to help you. Include information about why you think the author made the choice to include this text feature.

It is OK if your book does not have all of the features listed. It may still be a high-quality book even if it does not have all of these features.

Book Title: ______________________ **Author:** ______________________

Main Topic: ______________________

Features		Yes	No
Table of Contents and/or Chapter Titles *Hint: Look in the front of the book.*	What are some of the main topics of the book, based on the table of contents or chapter titles?		
Index and/or Glossary *Hint: Look in the back of the book.*	What are some of the important words or topics this book will tell you about?		
Headings *Hint: Look for a few words that introduce different sections or parts of the book/chapter.*	What can you tell about how the book/chapter is organized based on the headings?		
Bold or Italic Text	What kinds of words or information does the author highlight by using bold or italic text?		

Features		Yes	No
Drawings, Photographs, or Maps *Including captions.*	What kinds of pictures are included? What can you tell about the topics of the book/chapter from the pictures?		
Graphs, Charts, or Tables *Including captions.*	What kind of information is presented in graphs, charts, and tables in the book/chapter?		
Other features you noticed: ________ ________			
Based on the features noted above, what predictions can you make about the book/chapter you are about to read?			

Note. Adapted from *Exploring Nonfiction: Questions and Organizers to Guide Teaching and Understanding Nonfiction Texts* (p. 5) by Center for Gifted Education, 2004, Williamsburg, VA: Author. Copyright 2004 by Center for Gifted Education. Adapted with permission.

NAME:______________________________ DATE:____________

Choices

LESSON 1.3

Learning About Lincoln

Directions: Complete the questions below on a separate sheet of paper.

1. Pages 1–6 briefly outline Lincoln's life from birth to his presidency. Write 3–4 sentences that would sequence these important life events.
2. How do you think the author feels about Lincoln before he was president and after he was president? What evidence from the text supports your ideas?
3. Based on your reading, how do you feel President Lincoln changed over the course of his life? How did he stay the same? Use textual evidence to support your thoughts.
4. How do the pictures in this book help to add to your understanding of Lincoln's life? Use a specific example from the book to help you answer this question.
5. How do the captions help to support your understanding of the text? Explain your thoughts using text evidence.
6. If you could add a text feature that is not present in this book, what would you add? Why would that addition help a reader to better understand the information in the book?

NAME:______________________________ DATE:______________

LESSON 1.3

Research Guide

Historical Figure:	**Lifespan:**
Major Accomplishments:	Early Life:
Why is this person important in history?	What choices made by this person can we learn from today?
Additional Notes:	

Choices

LESSON 1.4

Central Choices

Common Core State Standards

- RL.3.2
- RL.3.3
- RL.3.6
- W.3.1
- W.3.8
- W.3.10
- SL.3.1
- SL.3.4
- SL.3.6
- L.3.1
- L.3.2
- L.3.3

Materials

- Lesson 1.4 Literature Analysis Model
- Lesson 1.4 Fables and Morals
- Lesson 1.4 Fable Brainstorming
- Computer and Internet access
- Sticky notes
- Teacher's copy of *Shared Inquiry Handbook of Discussion Leaders and Participants* (http://www.greatbooks.org/wp-content/uploads/2014/12/Shared-Inquiry-Handbook.pdf)

Estimated Time

- 120 minutes

Objectives

In this lesson, students will:

- recount stories (fables) from diverse cultures to determine the central message or moral and explain how it is conveyed through key details,
- describe characters in a story and explain how their actions contribute to the sequence of events in the story, and
- compose an original fable.

Content

Students will read several fables of their choice and identify the elements of fables in each one. Students will analyze the moral to determine its actual meaning and describe how the character's choices helped to develop the moral. Students will then create their own fable, using the mentor fables as a guide. Students will share fables with a partner and have the partner analyze the student-written fable for a moral.

Prior Knowledge

Students will need experience with fables and determining morals. Students will need to know the elements of fables.

INSTRUCTIONAL SEQUENCE

1. Explain to students that they will read four fables from http://read.gov/aesop/001.html (or another website or book of your choice) with a partner. Use the Shared Inquiry Guide (see Materials list) as one method for conducting a class discussion. For an initial analysis of one of the fables, work with students to complete Lesson 1.4 Literature Analysis Model. You may wish to select specific boxes for students to complete, based on your emphases for this lesson. (See pp. 3–4 for additional information about using the Literature Analysis Model.)
2. As they read, groups will complete a chart on fables and answer a series of questions regarding the fables chosen (see Lesson 1.4 Fables and Morals).
3. Discuss the role of choice in these fables. Guiding questions may include:
   - How does having a choice play a role in these fables?
   - Why does making a choice provide the possibility for having a moral for a story?
   - In which cases did the characters make good choices? Bad ones?

4. Next, have students compose their own fable. Students will use the fables they just read as mentor texts, as well as their prior knowledge of fable elements. Prior to writing, have students address the following questions:
   - What are the essential elements of a fable? (You will want students to understand that they are fictional, brief, usually have no more than three or four characters, usually have animals who are in conflict with each other as characters, have just one main event, and have a lesson stated at the end as a moral.)
   - Why are fables a powerful way of teaching a lesson?

5. Have students complete Lesson 1.4 Fable Brainstorming prior to writing their stories. Allow students time to compose their fables and get comments from you or their peers on the writing process.
6. Ask students to trade fables with a partner. Partners will read each other's fables and analyze the text to determine the moral. Students should record their thoughts about the fable on a sticky note and place this on their partner's fable so that they can see if they agree when they return the fable to its author.

Teacher's Note. Instead of trading with a partner, students could place their fables on desks around the room and circulate, leaving their thoughts about the moral on a sticky note at each fable they visit.

Extension Activities

Students may:

- rewrite one of the fables from the first person point of view of one of the characters, using this perspective to justify the choices made by a character in a traditional fable, or
- create a play based on their original fable or one of the mentor text fables. Allow students to perform the play for the class or parents.

NAME:____ DATE:_______________

LESSON 1.4

Literature Analysis Model

Directions: Complete this Literature Analysis Model about the fable you read.

	Chosen or Assigned Text: ____________________
Key Words	
Important Ideas	
Tone	
Mood	
Imagery	
Symbolism	
Structure of Writing	

Note. Adapted from *Exploring America in the 1950s* (p. 10) by M. Sandling & K. L. Chandler, 2014, Waco, TX: Prufrock Press. Copyright 2014 by Center for Gifted Education. Adapted with permission.

NAME:______________________________ DATE:______________

LESSON 1.4
Fables and Morals

Directions: Read four fables and analyze the moral based on the character's actions that led to the development of the moral. Complete the following chart as you read your four fables. Then, answer the questions with your partner.

Fable Title	Moral	Actual Meaning of Moral	Choice(s) Made by Character(s)	Character Actions That Lead to Moral

1. What connections could be made between the moral and the events of the fable?

2. What connections could be made between the moral and the natural traits and physical attributes of the animals seen in the fables?

3. All of the characters in the fables you read made certain choices. Choose one choice made by one character from each fable and explain how that choice led to the moral of the fable.

4. Would you make the same choices if you were in these characters' places? Why?

5. Imagine that in all fables characters always made good choices. How would the morals change?

NAME:______________________________ DATE:______________

LESSON 1.4

Fable Brainstorming

Directions: Complete the chart below as you brainstorm your ideas for a fable.

Setting:	
Character 1:	Character Traits:
	Details to Support Traits:
Character 2:	Character Traits:
	Details to Support Traits:
Character 3:	Character Traits:
	Details to Support Traits:
Problem:	
Resolution:	
Moral:	

NAME:______________________________ DATE:______________

UNIT I

Culminating Essay Prompt

Directions: In this unit, you read about different people and characters making choices. Describe what you have learned about making choices. Discuss how the choices made by a person or character affect that person or character.

UNIT II

Culture

This unit centers on the ideas related to the cultures of different people of the world; how cultures affect people, authors, and characters; and how cultures can cause people and characters to grow over time. Within the unit, students will read, analyze, evaluate, and interpret poetry, short stories, and nonfiction texts with themes related to culture and the effects of that culture on those who are part of it. They will consider the cultures of global neighbors, authors, characters, and themselves as they work to develop a deeper understanding of culture in literature and nonfiction. Students will demonstrate their growing understanding of this theme through various projects, informational writing, and poetry.

LESSON 2.1

Cultural Traditions?

Common Core State Standards

- RL. 3.10
- RF.3.3
- RF.3.4
- W.3.4
- W.3.10
- SL.3.1
- SL.3.2
- SL.3.3
- SL.3.6
- L.3.1
- L.3.2
- L.3.3
- L.3.6

Materials

- Lesson 2.1 Culture in Cinderella Stories
- Lesson 2.1 Literature Analysis Model
- Lesson 2.1 Exploring Giovanni Poetry
- Lesson 2.1 Culture Poem Brainstorming
- Lesson 2.1 Rubric: Exploring Giovanni Poetry
- Teacher's copy of a traditional version of "Cinderella" (to display)
- Teacher's copy of "Cinderella" from another culture (there are many, including Chinese, Egyptian, Caribbean, Persian, African, and Mexican versions; to display)
- Student copies of "Knoxville, Tennessee" by Nikki Giovanni

Estimated Time

- 90–120 minutes

Objectives

In this lesson, students will:

- read and analyze variations of the classic Cinderella story to determine how culture can be shown differently in literature from various parts of the world,
- analyze poetry while collaborating with peers during literary discussions, and
- create an original poem about the qualities of his or her culture.

Content

Students will read and analyze Cinderella stories from various cultures to gain an understanding of what "culture" entails. Students will analyze a poem in order to determine how the author uses language to create imagery in the reader's mind, as well as how the author uses parts of speech to effectively describe the culture of an area of our country.

Prior Knowledge

Students will need to know and understand how to identify stanzas and lines in pieces of poetry. Students will also need to know the basic parts of speech (nouns, verbs, and adverbs) and how each work in the structure of a sentence. Students will need to be aware of poetry terms, such as imagery.

Teacher's Note. This lesson might best be used after a unit that teaches the various parts of speech. This lesson serves as a meaningful method of assessment in which application of the parts of speech is integrated in writing, as opposed to isolated assessment of skills.

INSTRUCTIONAL SEQUENCE

1. Share a traditional version of "Cinderella." Then share a version of the story that represents a different culture. Have students use Lesson 2.1 Culture in Cinderella Stories to delineate some of the cultural differences in the stories. Explain to students that one definition of culture is the combination of information, beliefs, and behavior that people learn and pass on to their family members in future generations. People express their cultures in certain ways, such as clothing, food, and holiday traditions. Ask:
   - What are the similarities between the two stories?
   - What are the differences between the two stories?
   - What are examples of cultural differences that you see in the two stories?
   - How does a culture use literature to express its culture?

2. Have students to turn to a partner and tell about their traditional summer activities. Ask:
   - What are some of your family's traditional summer activities?
   - Do any of these activities specifically reflect your cultural heritage? How? (Explain that the selection they will be reading will reflect a Southern cultural heritage enjoyed by some people who live in the Southern part of the United States.)
   - What do the adults in your family tell you about the way the family does certain things at certain times of year or during holidays?
   - How does your family express its culture?

3. Continue by reading the poem "Knoxville, Tennessee" by Nikki Giovanni aloud while students follow along. For an initial analysis, work with students to complete Lesson 2.1 Literature Analysis Model. You may wish to have students complete specific boxes that will be the focus of this lesson.
4. Have students read the poem again with a partner. Then, facilitate a discussion using the following questions (answers will vary):
   - Nikki Giovanni uses many words and phrases to create imagery in the mind of the reader. What images came to your mind when you read this poem? (Students may mention picturing gardens, food, church, or mountains.)

- Based on what you read in the poem, what do you think summer is like for children in Knoxville, TN? (Students may mention that summer seems to be centered around outside due to the reference to the gardens, mountains, and warm weather.)
- How does this compare to some of the traditional summer activities in your region?
- What are some other traditional activities unique to your region for other seasons of the year? How might this be different from your prior knowledge about seasonal traditions in different places in the world?

5. Students will write a poem in the style of Nikki Giovanni's "Knoxville, Tennessee" about cultural traditions they enjoy during a particular season of the year. They will need to analyze Nikki Giovanni's writing style before they begin. Encourage students to look at the repetition at the beginning of lines, the brevity of the lines, the lack of rhyme scheme, and the fact that there is only one stanza. Guiding questions are included on Lesson 2.1 Exploring Giovanni Poetry.
6. Allow students time to discuss with their partners Nikki Giovanni's writing style. Have students use Lesson 2.1 Culture Poem Brainstorming to plan for their poem writing. Show students Lesson 2.1 Rubric: Exploring Giovanni Poetry before they begin writing.
7. Students can share poems with classmates once finished or publish them in class book. You may want students to use a web-publishing tool, such as http://www.storybird.com.

Extension Activities

Students may:

- record themselves reading their poetry and include images that also represent their culture,
- create an original dance and music to accompany their poem and perform it for students or parents, or
- research cultural seasonal traditions from around the world and present their findings to the class.

NAME:______________________ DATE:____________

LESSON 2.1

Culture in Cinderella Stories

Directions: After listening to each version of "Cinderella," complete this chart in preparation for a class discussion about culture.

Traditional Version	____________ Version
Clothing:	Clothing:
Homes/Shelter:	Homes/Shelter:
Food:	Food:
Behavior:	Behavior:
Government:	Government:
Geography:	Geography:
Work:	Work:
Recreation:	Recreation:
Customs:	Customs:
Information revealed about the culture:	Information revealed about the culture:

NAME:______________________________ DATE:______________

LESSON 2.1
Literature Analysis Model

Directions: Complete this Literature Analysis Model about "Knoxville, Tennessee" by Nikki Giovanni.

	"Knoxville, Tennessee" by Nikki Giovanni
Key Words	
Important Ideas	
Tone	
Mood	
Imagery	
Symbolism	
Structure of Writing	

Note. Adapted from *Exploring America in the 1950s* (p. 10) by M. Sandling & K. L. Chandler, 2014, Waco, TX: Prufrock Press. Copyright 2014 by Center for Gifted Education. Adapted with permission.

NAME:______________________________________ DATE:__________________

Culture

LESSON 2.1

Exploring Giovanni Poetry

Directions: With a partner, discuss and answer the questions on a separate sheet of paper, using Nikki Giovanni's poem, "Knoxville, Tennessee."

1. How has the author used imagery to help you understand life in Knoxville, TN?
2. What are some effective nouns and adjectives that help support the imagery you discussed in Question 1?
3. How do most lines begin? How is repetition used to create a certain rhythm in the poem?
4. How do the lengths of each line add to the message the author wants to send through this poem?
5. Does the author have a rhyme scheme in this poem? How might working in this style help the author focus on her message?
6. How might this poem be different if the poem was broken into multiple stanzas? Would the rhythm of the poem by the same? Would the author's message be as powerful?

NAME:______________________ DATE:______________

LESSON 2.1

Culture Poem Brainstorming

Directions: Use the left column of the chart to brainstorm ideas about your culture and how it affects your activities and your life. Use the right column of the chart to brainstorm ideas about how you could include that in your poem.

My Culture	
Cultural Elements	**What I Could Include In My Poem**
Clothing:	Clothing:
Homes/Shelter:	Homes/Shelter:
Food:	Food:
Behavior:	Behavior:
Government:	Government:
Geography:	Geography:
Work:	Work:
Recreation:	Recreation:
Customs:	Customs:
Information revealed about the culture:	Information revealed about the culture:

NAME:______________________________ DATE:______________

Culture

LESSON 2.1 RUBRIC

Exploring Giovanni Poetry

	Exceeds Expectations 5 points	Proficient 4 points	Developed 3 points	Emerging 2 points	Novice 1 point
Ideas in Poem	Created in the style of Nikki Giovanni's "Knoxville, Tennessee" and uses personal details to describe unique cultural traditions of specific seasons.	Created in the style of Nikki Giovanni's "Knoxville, Tennessee" and uses personal details to describe cultural traditions of a specific season.	Created in the style of Nikki Giovanni's "Knoxville, Tennessee" and uses personal details that do not really describe cultural traditions of a specific season.	Created in the style of Nikki Giovanni's "Knoxville, Tennessee" while using many similar ideas to the mentor poem.	Not created in the style of Nikki Giovanni's "Knoxville, Tennessee."
Descriptive Language	Contains correct use of all of the following parts of speech used in a manner that clearly creates imagery in the mind of the reader: pronoun, adjective, irregular plural noun, possessive noun, and abstract noun.	Contains correct use of all of the following parts of speech: pronoun, adjective, irregular plural noun, possessive noun, and abstract noun.	Contains correct use of at least four of the following parts of speech: pronoun, adjective, irregular plural noun, possessive noun, and abstract noun.	Contains correct use of at least three of the following parts of speech: pronoun, adjective, irregular plural noun, possessive noun, and abstract noun.	Contains correct use of two or less of the following parts of speech: pronoun, adjective, irregular plural noun, possessive noun, and abstract noun.
Poem Structure	Written in free verse, with no particular rhyme scheme or stanzas, but has an original quality to the poem.	Written in free verse, with no particular rhyme scheme or stanzas.	Missing one of the following: free verse form, absence of rhyme scheme, or absence of stanzas.	Missing two of the following: free verse form, absence of rhyme scheme, or absence of stanzas.	Shows minimal effort toward replication of the mentor poem's structure.
Conventions	Demonstrates superior command of the conventions of the English language, with no errors in grammar, spelling, or usage.	Demonstrates command of the conventions of the English language, with no more than one error in grammar, spelling, or usage.	Demonstrates command of the conventions of the English language, with no more than two errors in grammar, spelling, or usage.	Demonstrates command of the conventions of the English language, with no more than three errors in grammar, spelling, or usage.	Demonstrates novice command of the conventions of the English language, with more than three errors in grammar, spelling, or usage.
					________ / 16

LESSON 2.2

Are We All the Same?

Common Core State Standards

- RI.3.1
- RI.3.2
- RI.3.3
- RI.3.7
- RI.3.8
- RI.3.10
- W.3.7
- W.3.8
- W.3.10
- L.3.1
- L.3.2
- L.3.3

Materials

- Lesson 2.2 World Village Exploration
- Lesson 2.2 Planning Chart
- Lesson 2.2 Reading Log
- Lesson 2.2 Question Charts
- Lesson 2.2 Rubric: World Village Brochure
- *If the World Were a Village* by David Smith (http://www.slideshare.net/PriscillaChu/if-the-world-were-a-village-13379766)

Estimated Time

- 100 minutes

Objectives

In this lesson, students will:

- analyze nonfiction texts in order to compare and contrast the most important points and key details presented in two texts on the same topic,
- research to gain knowledge on a specified topic, and
- create a brochure to demonstrate knowledge gained from research.

Content

Students will read a nonfiction text that speculates on how things would be if the world were the size of a village. Students will work to discover the main idea of the text, explain how illustrations contribute to the meaning of the text, and determine the meaning of words using context clues.

Prior Knowledge

Students will need experience researching independently or with partners. Students will need guidance on how to gain information from online resources. Students will also need to be familiar with terminology of nonfiction text features.

INSTRUCTIONAL SEQUENCE

1. Ask students what they know about the world outside of their city, state, and country, activating prior knowledge. Consider creating an anchor chart of student responses and add to it after the lesson.
2. Explain to students that they will work with a partner to read *If the World Were a Village* by David Smith. While reading, they will answer questions on Lesson 2.2 World Village Exploration.
3. Afterward, have a discussion on questions raised. Ask students if they learned about an area or country about which they would like to learn more. Allow students to develop questions based on interest piqued during reading. Students will use these questions to guide their research for their final brochure. Guiding questions may include:
   - What did you find interesting during your reading?
   - Did you notice anything that you would like to learn more about?
   - Do your questions all have only one correct answer? If so, you may want to see about rewording your question so that multiple answers would be correct.
   - How could learning more about your topic help you learn more about a culture other than yours?

Teacher's Note. Explain that students will need to conduct a short research project to learn more about their country using the website http://www.timeforkids.com (or one of your choosing) or nonfiction texts. You may want to assign countries if you want all of the countries to be researched during the lesson. You may also allow students to randomly draw names of countries to be studied.

4. Have students use metacognitive planners to assist them in reviewing various books or websites for their research. Lesson 2.2 Planning Chart requires students to make a plan for what they hope to learn from reading a book or using a website. Lesson 2.2 Reading Log is a way to record and evaluate information acquired from their book or website. Lesson 2.2 Question Charts helps students to think about what they are reading. They should use the questions they wrote in Lesson 2.2 Planning Chart to complete the first column. Then they should complete the other sections of the chart as they read.
5. Explain to students that they will need to use Lesson 2.2 World Village Brochure Rubric to create a brochure to demonstrate the knowledge gained from their research. You may want to allow students to use publishing software, such as Microsoft Publisher, to create their brochures.
6. Students will share their brochures with the class and then add them to the school library or display them elsewhere in the school.

Extension Activity

Students may:

- create a different form of visual presentation for their research, using the rubric as a guideline for research, such as a Weebly page, Voki, or travel blog.

NAME:________________________ DATE:____________

LESSON 2.2

World Village Exploration

Directions: Read *If the World Were a Village* by David Smith and discuss the text with a partner. Then work with your partner to answer the questions on this sheet to the best of your ability, using text evidence to support your claims.

1. What is the main idea of the text?

2. Based on the context clues provided by the text, what do you think the following words mean?

Word	Page Number	My Definition	Reason for My Definition	Actual Meaning of the Word
Population				
Village				
Global				
Babel				

Culture

Culture

3. On Page 12, Smith explains what happens to the population of a village as years pass and people grow older. Explain the comparison between the numbers of young versus old people in a village over the passage of time.

4. Hypothesize what would happen to the ratio of young to old if the average age to which people lived was increased by medicine to 110 years old. How would this affect the resources a village (or the world) would have available?

5. How do the illustrations in the book help you to better understand the text?

NAME:______________________________ DATE:______________

LESSON 2.2

Planning Chart

Directions: Plan what you hope to learn from reading your book or website. Complete the chart below.

I (or my teacher) chose this book because . . .	
The country I am studying is . . .	
My main reason for studying this country is . . .	
Two subtopics (or details) that I need to know about my country are . . .	
1.	**2.**
Two things I already know about my main topic or subtopics are . . .	
1.	**2.**

Culture

Three questions about my country that I want to find answers to are . . .		
1.	2.	3.

I think this book or website will help me with my topic because . . .

I think the author's purpose in writing this book or website was . . .

When I read this book or website, I will . . . (check one)	
_______ read it straight through from beginning to end.	_______ skim to find sections that will help me answer my questions.

While I read, I will use these features to help me understand the book or website and find the information I need . . .

Note. Adapted from *Exploring Nonfiction: Questions and Organizers to Guide Teaching and Understanding Nonfiction Texts* (p. 6) by Center for Gifted Education, 2004, Williamsburg, VA: Author. Copyright 2004 by Center for Gifted Education. Adapted with permission.

NAME:________________________ DATE:____________

LESSON 2.2

Reading Log

Directions: As you read, keep a reading log. In the left column, write interesting facts, new words, new ideas, and things you didn't know before. Write down the page number with each entry. Then, in the right column, write your personal reaction to each entry. Your personal reaction may be a sentence to answer one of these questions: Why did you choose to include the entry in your reading log? What was interesting about the entry? What new information did you learn from this detail? How does this idea tell you more about something you already knew about the topic?

New Information	Page Number	My Reaction

Note. Adapted from *Exploring Nonfiction: Questions and Organizers to Guide Teaching and Understanding Nonfiction Texts* (p. 8) by Center for Gifted Education, 2004, Williamsburg, VA: Author. Copyright 2004 by Center for Gifted Education. Adapted with permission.

NAME:_______________________________________ DATE:_______________

LESSON 2.2

Question Charts

Directions: Use these charts to help you think about what you are reading. Use the three questions you wrote in Lesson 2.2 Planning Chart to begin completing the first column. Then complete the other sections of the chart as you read.

Questions I Had Before Reading	Answers I Found	How I Found the Answer (Stated in the Text or a Conclusion I Drew)	Questions I Thought of While Reading

Culture

When you have finished reading, write some of the questions you still have with some ideas about where you might find the answers.

Questions I Still Have	How I Will Find the Answer

Note. Adapted from *Exploring Nonfiction: Questions and Organizers to Guide Teaching and Understanding Nonfiction Texts* (p. 9) by Center for Gifted Education, 2004, Williamsburg, VA: Author. Copyright 2004 by Center for Gifted Education. Adapted with permission.

NAME:____ DATE:_______________

LESSON 2.2 RUBRIC

World Village Brochure

Directions: Be sure to include and address the following in your brochure. Use this rubric to guide your research.

	Exceeds Expectations 9 points	Proficient 8 points	Developed 7 points	Emerging 6 points	Novice 5-0 points
Basic Information	Title clearly states the main research question, while subtitles indicate smaller guiding questions used in research in a creative and unique manner.	Title clearly states the main research question, while subtitles indicate smaller guiding questions used in research.	Title clearly states the main research question.	Hints at the questions used to guide the research.	Lacks an evident purpose behind the research.
Brochure Structure	Neat, creative, and inviting to the audience, with nonfiction text features to help organize the information presented.	Neat and inviting to the audience, with nonfiction text features to help organize the information presented.	Neat and uses nonfiction text features to help organize the information presented.	Uses nonfiction text features to help organize the information presented.	Unorganized and hard for the reader to gather information.
Conventions	Demonstrates superior command of the conventions of the English language, with no errors in grammar, spelling, or usage.	Demonstrates command of the conventions of the English language, with no more than one error in grammar, spelling, or usage.	Demonstrates command of the conventions of the English language, with no more than two errors in grammar, spelling, or usage.	Demonstrates command of the conventions of the English language, with no more than three errors in grammar, spelling, or usage.	Demonstrates novice command of the conventions of the English language, with more than three errors in grammar, spelling, or usage.
					________ / 24

Culture

LESSON 2.3

What Cultural Traditions Can Tell Us

Common Core State Standards

- RI.3.1
- RI.3.2
- RI.3.5
- RI.3.7
- RI.3.9
- RI.3.10
- W.3.2
- W.3.7
- W.3.8
- W.3.10
- L.3.1
- L.3.2
- L.3.3

Materials

- Lesson 2.3 Cultural Traditions
- Lesson 2.3 Three Circle Venn Diagram
- Teacher's and student copies of *Throw Your Tooth on the Roof* by Selby Beeler
- Student copies of *Art Around the World* by Heather Leonard
- Student copies of *What the World Eats* by Faith D'Aluisio

Estimated Time

- 90 minutes

Objectives

In this lesson, students will:

- analyze nonfiction texts, and
- create an informative essay using information gained from research while demonstrating command of the conventions of standard English grammar.

Content

Students will listen to *Throw Your Tooth on the Roof* by Selby Beeler and compare traditions of what to do with a lost tooth in cultures around the world to their own traditions. Students will then read two other nonfiction texts that illustrate other aspects of world cultures in order to make a comparison to their own culture. The lesson will end with students writing a culminating essay comparing two cultural traditions and customs from cultures around the world.

Prior Knowledge

Students will need experience using text features such as headings, subheadings, captions, and indexes in order to better gain required information.

INSTRUCTIONAL SEQUENCE

1. Read *Throw Your Tooth on the Roof* by Selby Beeler aloud.
2. Distribute copies of the book to small groups or pairs. Have students use Lesson 2.3 Cultural Traditions to organize the information gained during reading. This information will be used for the final culminating essay of the lesson.

Teacher's Note. Students may also use the reading of *Throw Your Tooth on the Roof* on YouTube if enough copies of Beeler's book are not available.

- Part I: https://www.youtube.com/watch?v=Rx4vIOsr69M
- Part II: https://www.youtube.com/watch?v=LHV4ReeXwC4
- Part III: https://www.youtube.com/watch?v=xtX8pvhJS8Q

You may also choose to discuss the questions on Lesson 2.3 Cultural Traditions with students as a whole group after or during the class reading before moving to the group work part of the lesson.

3. Have students work with a partner to read two related texts, *Art Around the World* and *What the World Eats*, to explore other cultural traditions. Students will use Lesson 2.3 Cultural Traditions to organize their findings.
4. Have students write an essay comparing and contrasting two cultures according to common traditions or customs, using the three texts to support their thoughts. Have students use Lesson 2.3 Three Circle Venn Diagram to organize their thinking.

Teacher's Note. You can increase the complexity of this lesson in the essay requirements by not allowing students to use their own culture or by increasing the number of cultures compared and contrasted in the essay.

Extension Activities

Students may:

- research a different tradition around the world that interests them to use as additional support for their essay, or
- discuss and create generalizations regarding what defines *culture*, using their research as support for their argument.

NAME:____ DATE:____________________

LESSON 2.3

Cultural Traditions

Directions: Use the graphic organizer below to organize your knowledge gained from the informational texts you have read. Then discuss the following questions with your partner to extend your thinking. You will use this information to compose an essay in which you will compare and contrast various cultural traditions and customs around the world.

Guiding Question	*Throw Your Tooth on the Roof* by Selby Beeler	*Art Around the World* by Heather Leonard	*What the World Eats* by Faith D'Aluisio
How are the cultural traditions or customs presented in this book similar to your cultural traditions or customs?			
How are the cultural traditions or customs presented in this book different from your cultural traditions or customs?			
How do the illustrations in this book help support the differences and similarities between cultural traditions or customs?			

Culture

Extend Your Thinking

1. Why do you think traditions vary so much from culture to culture?

2. Does the geography have any connection to similarities and differences between cultures?

3. Do you notice any underlying similarities between traditions or customs among the cultures researched today? What may these similarities be?

NAME:______________________________ DATE:______________

LESSON 2.3

Three Circle Venn Diagram

Directions: Use this three circle Venn diagram to help organize your thoughts for the comparative essay. Then, write an essay comparing and contrasting two cultures according to common traditions or customs. Be sure to use information from all three texts to support your thoughts.

Text 1: ______________ Text 2: ______________

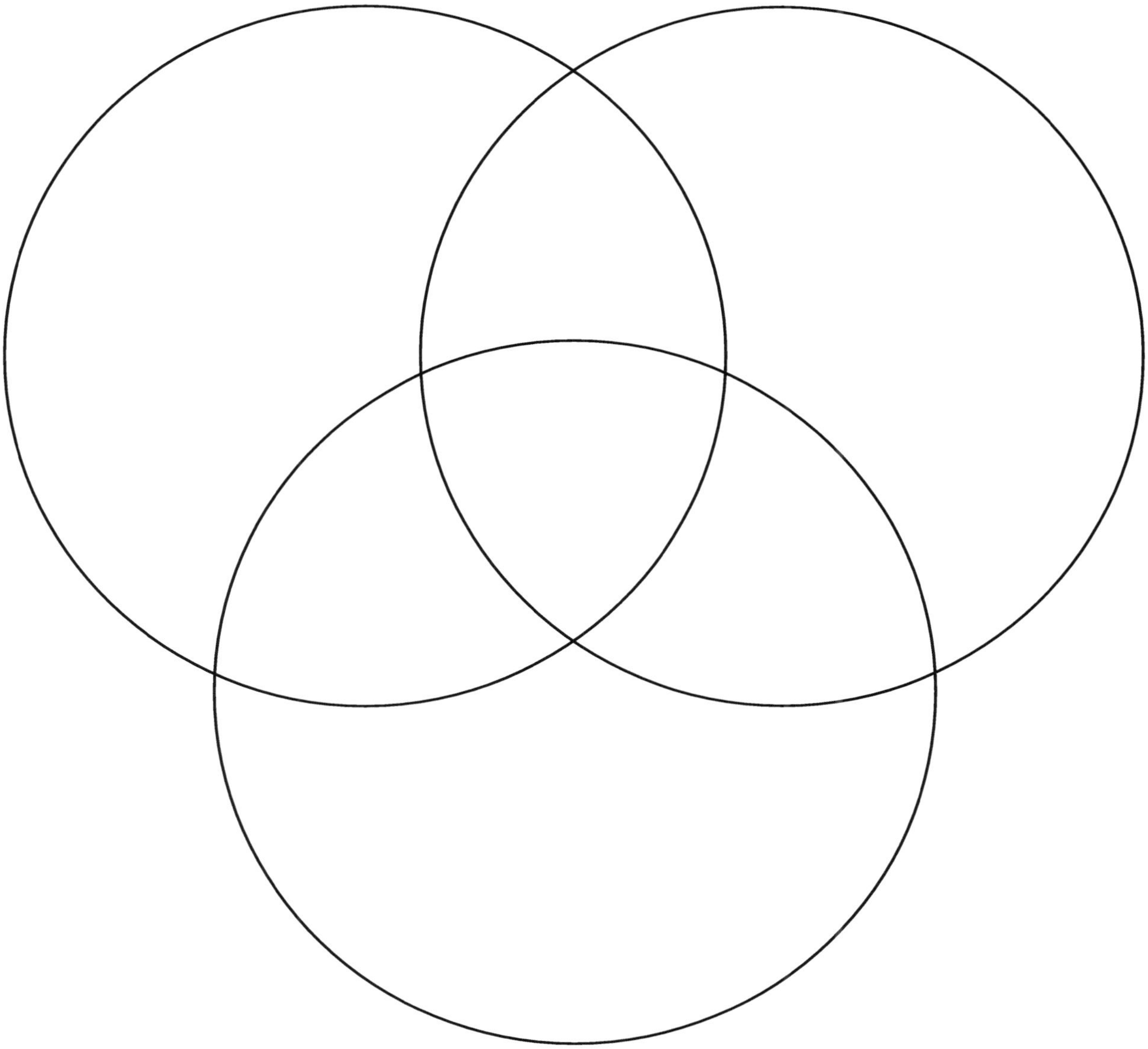

Text 3: ______________

Culture

LESSON 2.4

Cultures of the Past

Common Core State Standards

- RI.3.4
- RI.3.7
- RI.3.8
- W.3.2
- W.3.4
- W.3.7
- W.3.8
- W.3.10
- SL.3.1
- SL.3.2
- SL.3.6
- L.3.1
- L.3.2
- L.3.3
- L.3.4

Materials

- Lesson 2.4 Medieval Feast
- Lesson 2.4 Rubric: Medieval Feast Invitation
- *Medieval Feast* by Aliki
- Student copies of "The Middle Ages–Medieval Castles" by ReadWorks.org (http://www.readworks.org/passages/middle-ages-medieval-castles)
- Video reading of *Medieval Feast* by Aliki (http://www.watchknowlearn.org/Video.aspx?VideoID=36327&CategoryID=10501)
- Picture of a medieval feast
- Computer and Internet access

Estimated Time

- 120 minutes

Objectives

In this lesson, students will:

- analyze nonfiction texts, and
- create an original and authentic invitation using knowledge gained from research.

Content

Students will read two informational texts about the medieval times to develop a better understanding of the culture of the time period. Students will synthesize their knowledge of the culture of the time period to develop an invitation to their own medieval feast. Students will need to include information about various aspects of the culture and cultural expectations on the invitation to make it authentic to that time period.

Prior Knowledge

Students will need experience using context clues in determining the meaning of unfamiliar words or phrases in a piece of nonfiction text. Students will also need to be able to use what they have read along with prior knowledge to make inferences.

INSTRUCTIONAL SEQUENCE

1. Display a picture of a medieval feast and have students write down ideas about what is going on in the picture. Have students share their thoughts, using evidence from the picture. If an image cannot be found, you can show the cover of *Medieval Feast* by Aliki.
2. Explain to students that they will read a nonfiction text about medieval castles in order to gain a better understanding of the cultural setting of the picture.
3. Students will read independently or with a partner "The Middle Ages—Medieval Castles" and answer the accompanying questions on the ReadWorks.org passage.
4. Students will then watch a video on WatchKnowLearn.org of a reading of Aliki's *Medieval Feast*. Explain that as they watch, they should use the words and the pictures to help them develop an understanding of what was important to the culture in that time period.
5. Then, have them answer questions on Lesson 2.4 Medieval Feast, referring to the texts for support for their answers.
6. After students have compared the two texts, ask:
   - What are some examples of feasts that we have in our culture?
   - What are the characteristics that cause something to be considered a "feast"?
   - What types of foods has your family had at one of your feasts? Describe special activities that are done at this feast. Describe how people act and dress at this feast.
   - How is your "feast" similar to and different from the medieval feast?
   - What can traditions seen at your "feast" and a medieval feast tell us about the culture of that time period?

7. Explain to students that with their better understanding of the cultural expectations of the time period, they are to develop an invitation to a medieval feast. They will need to refer to Lesson 2.4 Rubric: Medieval Feast Invitation for details on what must be included.

Extension Activities

Students may:

- host a medieval feast for family members (this would be a great crosscurricular connection, as tasks from all subject areas would be included),
- complete research on other aspects of medieval life and present their findings to their classmates in an interactive format, or
- make a comparison of the medieval feast to a traditional "feast" in their own culture (e.g., Thanksgiving, birthday parties, family reunions). Have students then create their own book in the style of the mentor text to represent their own cultural feast.

NAME:______________________________ DATE:______________

LESSON 2.4

Medieval Feast

Directions: Read the nonfiction text provided and discuss the text with your partner. Work with your partner to answer the questions on this sheet to the best of your ability, always using text evidence to support your claims.

1. Based on the context clues provided by the text, what do you think the following words or phrases mean?

Word/Phrase	Page Number	My Definition	Reason for My Definition	Actual Meaning of the Word
Marzipan				
Turned on Spits				
Member of His Court				
Embroidered				
Estate				

Culture

Culture

2. Based on the context clues provided by the text, how would you describe the following social class/job?

Social Class/Job	Page Number	My Thoughts	Reason for My Thoughts	Actual Explanation of Social Class/Job
Serf				
Ewerer				
Scullion boy				

3. Why do you think there may have been certain classes of people? What might have separated these classes of people?

4. Sequence the preparations required for hosting a medieval feast based off of what you learned from the text. Be sure to include sequencing words.

5. Based on the preparations required for a medieval feast, how do you think the culture valued mealtimes? How might this be different than mealtimes in our culture?

6. Use the article "The Middle Ages–Medieval Castles" and Aliki's *Medieval Feast* to help you answer the following.
   a. Why might the kitchen in a medieval castle be separate from the main living areas?

   b. Besides the fact that there were ample amounts of fine food and gold vessels in the dining hall, how else could you tell the dining hall in Aliki's *Medieval Feast* belonged to a wealthy person?

7. How could you compare and contrast today's culture with a medieval culture?

NAME:____ DATE:________________

LESSON 2.4 RUBRIC

Medieval Feast Invitation

	Exceeds Expectations 9 points	Proficient 8 points	Developed 7 points	Emerging 6 points	Novice 5–0 points
Invitation Content	Includes the following content in a unique, creative manner that is not list-like: • reason for feast, • guests who may be in attendance, • service personnel who will be expected at the feast, • at least two menu items a guest may enjoy at the feast, • required attire for the feast, • times for the feast, and • directions to the feast.	Includes the following content in a manner that is not list-like: • reason for feast, • guests who may be in attendance, • service personnel who will be expected at the feast, • at least two menu items a guest may enjoy at the feast, • required attire for the feast, • times for the feast, and • directions to the feast.	Includes the following content in a list-like manner: • reason for feast, • guests who may be in attendance, • service personnel who will be expected at the feast, • at least two menu items a guest may enjoy at the feast, • required attire for the feast, • times for the feast, and • directions to the feast.	Missing no more than two of the following: • reason for feast, • guests who may be in attendance, • service personnel who will be expected at the feast, • at least two menu items a guest may enjoy at the feast, • required attire for the feast, • times for the feast, and • directions to the feast.	Missing three or more of the following (1 point off for each missing content element): • reason for feast, • guests who may be in attendance, • service personnel who will be expected at the feast, • at least two menu items a guest may enjoy at the feast, • required attire for the feast, • times for the feast, and • directions to the feast.
	Exceeds Expectations 5 points	**Proficient 4 points**	**Developed 3 points**	**Emerging 2 points**	**Novice 1 points**
Invitation Structure	Clearly welcoming to the recipient; neat and unique in showing the student's personality.	Clearly welcoming to the recipient; neat.	Clearly welcoming to the recipient.	Not welcoming in the design and may be confusing to the recipient.	Looks rushed and does not clearly state the purpose for the recipient.
Conventions	Demonstrates superior command of the conventions of the English language, with no errors in grammar, spelling, or usage.	Demonstrates command of the conventions of the English language, with no more than one error in grammar, spelling, or usage.	Demonstrates command of the conventions of the English language, with no more than two errors in grammar, spelling, or usage.	Demonstrates command of the conventions of the English language, with no more than three errors in grammar, spelling, or usage.	Demonstrates novice command of the conventions of the English language, with more than three errors in grammar, spelling, or usage.
					________ / 16

LESSON 2.5

Can Cultures Change a Person?

Common Core State Standards

- RL.3.1
- RL.3.2
- RL.3.3
- RL.3.5
- RL.3.7
- RL.3.10
- W.3.3
- W.3.10
- SL.3.1
- SL.3.2
- SL.3.6
- L.3.1
- L.3.2
- L.3.3
- L.3.4

Materials

- Lesson 2.5 Literature Analysis Model
- Lesson 2.5 Cultures and Change
- Teacher's copy of *The Raft* by Jim LaMarche
- Teacher's copy of *A Long Way From Chicago* by Richard Peck (optional)

Estimated Time

- 90 minutes

Objectives

In this lesson, students will:

- analyze fictional literature;
- determine how culture can affect a character's thoughts, words, and actions; and
- compose an original essay regarding changes in a character over the course of a fictional story.

Content

Students will analyze the characters in *The Raft* by Jim LaMarche to understand how characters' thoughts, feelings, and actions can change according to the culture surrounding them. Students will use their knowledge to write an essay on how culture changed a character's views or how being immersed in a different culture has changed their own viewpoints.

Prior Knowledge

Students will need to have read or have heard *The Raft* at least once before this lesson. Students will need experience determining the central message from texts, using illustrations to better understand text, and analyzing characters for traits, motivations, and feelings.

INSTRUCTIONAL SEQUENCE

1. Tell students that they are going to revisit a familiar story to deeply analyze characters and how the culture presented by the author affected the characters. Show students *The Raft* by Jim LaMarche. Briefly discuss the central message, plot, and characters of the story (a great summary is available at http://www.scholastic.com/teachers/book/raft#cart/cleanup). The discussion should elicit responses such as the following:
   - **Central messages:** Cleverness, creativity and imagination, and cultural differences.
   - **Plot and characters:** A young boy (Nicky) goes to spend the summer with his "river-rat" grandmother in a rural area. He is very upset about this at the start of the story, until he finds a raft on the river. Throughout the summer, he has adventures and begins to enjoy himself in this new environment. Over time, his opinions change as the "river" culture becomes a part of him.

2. Work with students to complete Lesson 2.5 Literature Analysis Model. (See pp. 3–4 for additional information about using the Literature Analysis Model.) Direct their attention to the cultural setting of the story. Explain that they need to try to describe the culture of Grandma's world and how it is different from Nicky's world. (Students should realize that Grandma's culture is different than Nicky's because Grandma lives in a rural area as opposed to the city Nicky is used to. Grandma's culture values nature, outdoors, and using your imagination to have fun.)
3. Allow students time to discuss this with small groups or partners. While students are discussing, walk around and help extend discussions where necessary and facilitate them where needed.
4. Afterward, explain to students that they will answer some questions to help organize their thoughts to prepare for an essay. Distribute Lesson 2.5 Cultures and Change. Allow students time to discuss and answer questions, using the text to support their thoughts.
5. Have students write an essay describing how being exposed to Grandma's culture changed Nicky's point of view. As an alternative, students can use the knowledge gained in this lesson to write an essay about how being immersed in a different culture has changed their own viewpoints.

Extension Activities

Students may:

- change *The Raft* into a play and perform it for their class, or
- compose a song from Nicky's perspective of how his view on culture changed from the beginning to the end of *The Raft*.

NAME:_______________________________ DATE:_______________

LESSON 2.5

Literature Analysis Model

Directions: Complete this Literature Analysis Model about *The Raft* by Jim LaMarche.

	***The Raft* by Jim La Marche**
Key Words	
Important Ideas	
Tone	
Mood	
Imagery	
Symbolism	
Structure of Writing	

Note. Adapted from *Exploring America in the 1950s* (p. 10) by M. Sandling & K. L. Chandler, 2014, Waco, TX: Prufrock Press. Copyright 2014 by Center for Gifted Education. Adapted with permission.

Culture

NAME:______________________________ DATE:______________

LESSON 2.5

Cultures and Change

Directions: Read the story provided and discuss the text while reading with your partner. Then work with your partner to answer the questions on this sheet to the best of your ability, always using text evidence to support your claims.

1. What would you consider the central message of the story to be?

2. How does Nicky's character help support the central message from the beginning of the story to the end of the story?

3. Describe the culture with which Nicky is familiar at the beginning of the story.

4. How is Grandma's culture different than Nicky's?

5. How do Grandma's actions throughout the story help to bring about a change in Nicky?

NAME:____ DATE:________________

UNIT II

Culminating Essay Prompt

Directions: In this unit, you read about different cultures and the role of culture in people's lives. Write about your personal definition of culture and then describe the parts of your family's culture that are most important to you.

UNIT III

Beliefs

This unit centers on the ideas related to the beliefs of various characters, authors, and historical figures and how those beliefs cause actions and growth in people and characters. Within the unit, students will read, analyze, evaluate, and interpret literature, novels, and nonfiction texts with themes related to beliefs and to the effects of a belief on those characters or historical figures. They will consider the beliefs of authors, characters, and themselves as they work to develop a deeper understanding of beliefs in literature and nonfiction. Students will demonstrate their growing understanding of this theme through various projects, narrative writing, informational writing, persuasive writing, and poetry.

LESSON 3.1

Belief in the Unknown

Common Core State Standards

- RI. 3.1
- RI.3.3
- RI.3.8
- RL.3.1
- RL.3.3
- W.3.3
- W.3.4
- W.3.5
- W.3.10
- SL.3.1
- SL.3.2
- SL.3.3
- SL.3.6
- L.3.1
- L.3.2
- L.3.3
- L.3.6

Materials

- Lesson 3.1 Exploring Myths
- Lesson 3.1 The Process of a Seed Becoming a Plant
- Lesson 3.1 Rubric: From Seed to Plant Myth
- *From Seed to Plant* by Gail Gibbons (http://www.watchknowlearn.org/Video.aspx?CategoryID=10502&VideoID=36335)
- Student copies of supplementary texts:
  - "Myths From Around the World: China" (http://teacher.scholastic.com/writewit/mff/china.htm)
  - "Pan Gu and Nü Wa" (http://www.gly.uga.edu/railsback/CS/CSPG&NW.html)
  - "Chinook Creation Myth" (http://quatr.us/northamerica/before1500/religion/chinook creation.htm)

Estimated Time

- 160 minutes

Objectives

In this lesson, students will:

- analyze nonfiction texts and traditional creation myths, and
- create an original myth to explain a natural process.

Content

Students will read creation myths to understand how ancient cultures tried to explain the origin of natural events that had no obvious explanation before the advent of modern science. Afterward, students will create a myth for how a seed becomes a plant based on prior knowledge of elements of myths. Students will read a nonfiction text in order to gain scientific knowledge behind a natural event. Students will then compare and contrast their myth with the scientific process.

Prior Knowledge

Students will need to be familiar with the myth genre and analyzing grade-level nonfiction texts.

INSTRUCTIONAL SEQUENCE

1. Ask students to quickly write all of the things they already know about the myth genre.
2. Explain that there are many myths about processes in the natural world that are now explainable by science. Before the advent of modern science, people created myths in order to explain their beliefs of why events in nature happened.
3. Tell students they are going to read one to three myths to see how they are structured. You can assign students a specific myth or have students explore all three myths in the alternative text selections. You may also incorporate other myths.
4. As students are exploring the myth(s), have them organize their thoughts using Lesson 3.1 Exploring Myths. Allow students to share and discuss their thoughts from the handout. If necessary, review the elements of the creation myth genre.
5. Have students imagine that they are members of an ancient culture and must create a myth to explain the process of a seed becoming a plant. They may use Lesson 3.1 Rubric: From Seed to Plant Myth to assist them.
6. After writing, students will investigate the scientific reason as to how a seed grows into a plant. Show students *From Seed to Plant* by Gail Gibbons and explain that they will work with a partner to read through this nonfiction text and answer a few questions.
7. Distribute Lesson 3.1 The Process of a Seed Becoming a Plant. Explain that now that students understand the scientific explanation of how a seed becomes a plant, they will compare and contrast their myth with the scientific explanation.
8. Allow students to share their thoughts from their Venn diagram on Lesson 3.1 The Process of a Seed Becoming a Plant with a partner.

Extension Activities

Students may:

- create a play or graphic novel to reflect their created myth;
- take an existing myth and write an informative essay to explain the process that happened, using scientific facts gained from research; or
- write a nonfiction essay comparing the two pieces of writing, their own myth, and *From Seed to Plant* by Gail Gibbons.

NAME:______________________________ DATE:______________

LESSON 3.1
Exploring Myths

Directions: As you read the myth(s) assigned to you, fill out the chart below to help to organize your thoughts.

Myth	Element of Nature	How Element of Nature Is Explained	Supernatural or Magical Characteristics
"Myths From Around the World: China"			
"Pan Gu and Nü Wa"			
"Chinook Creation Myth"			

Beliefs

NAME:________________________________ DATE:______________

LESSON 3.1

The Process of a Seed Becoming a Plant

Directions: Answer the following questions to the best of your ability, using the text to support your answers.

1. How does the process of a seed becoming a plant happening over time require belief in something that cannot be fully seen in a natural setting?

2. Using your knowledge from *From Seed to Plant* by Gail Gibbons, draw a representation of the life cycle of a plant.

3. Using sequencing words, write a step-by-step explanation of a seed becoming a plant.

4. How might people have described this phenomenon before the scientific reasons behind this process were discovered? Use your knowledge of the creation myth genre to help you answer this question.

5. Write two cause and effect statements using the knowledge gained from your reading.

6. Complete the Venn diagram to compare and contrast the scientific process of a seed becoming a plant to your myth of how a seed becomes a plant.

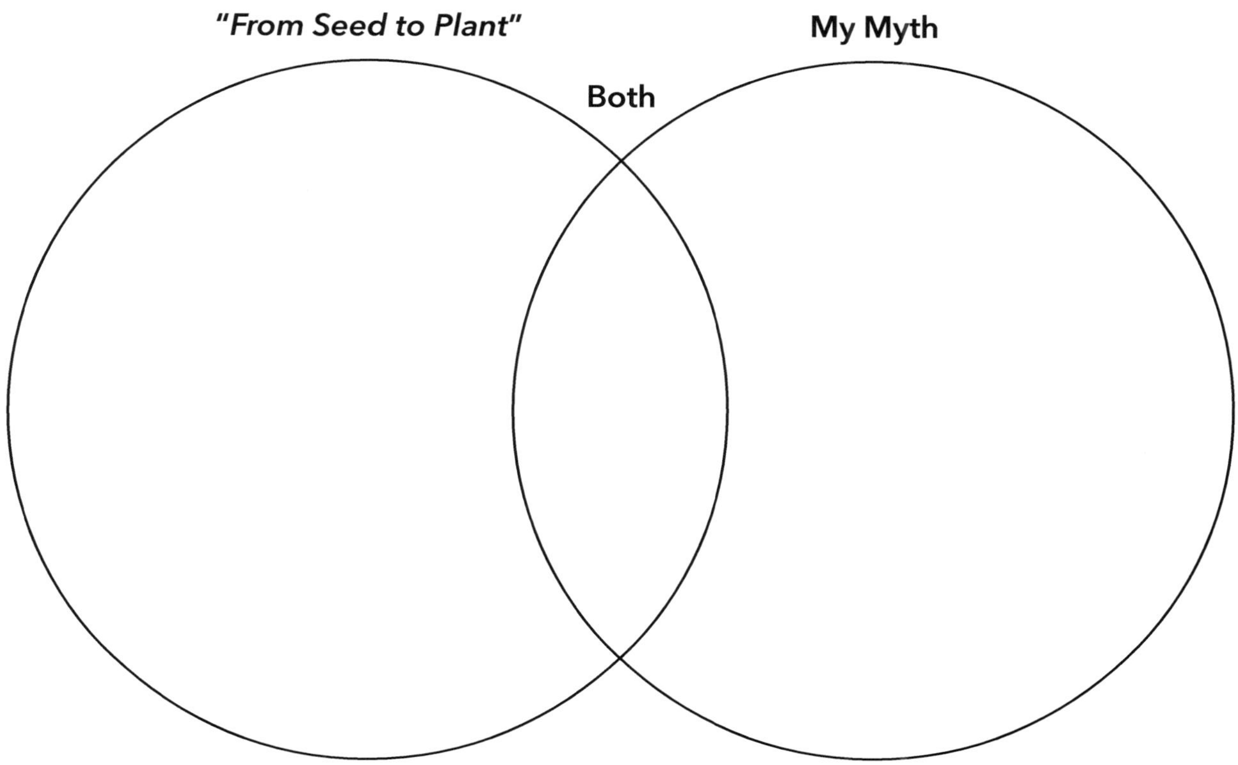

NAME:______________________________ DATE:____________

LESSON 3.1 RUBRIC

From Seed to Plant Myth

	Exceeds Expectations 5 points	Proficient 4 points	Developed 3 points	Emerging 2 points	Novice 1 point
Elements of the Creation Myth	Original and includes an explanation of the life cycle of a plant using the elements of myths as listed below: • gods/goddesses or supernatural beings, • magic, • change, • set in past, and • explanation for an element of nature.	Written in the style of one of the anchor myths and includes an explanation of the life cycle of a plant using the elements of myths as listed below: • gods/goddesses or supernatural beings, • magic, • change, • set in past, and • explanation for an element of nature.	Written in the style of one of the anchor myths, using the elements of myths as listed below: • gods/goddesses or supernatural beings, • magic, • change, • set in past, and • explanation for an element of nature.	Written in the style of one of the anchor myths, using at least three of the elements of myths as listed below: • gods/goddesses or supernatural beings, • magic, • change, • set in past, or • explanation for an element of nature.	The myth is written in the style of one of the anchor myths using fewer than two of the elements of myths as listed below: • gods/goddesses or supernatural beings, • magic, • change, • set in past, or • explanation for an element of nature.
Point of View and Word Choice	Written from third-person point of view with descriptive word choice.	Written from third-person point of view.	Written from third-person point of view with vague word choice.	Not written in third person, but has descriptive word choice.	Not written in third person and does not include descriptive word choice.
Ideas in Myth	Life cycle of a plant is clear with evidence as to how a plant grows that would be seen in the myth genre.	Life cycle of a plant is present with evidence as to how a plant grows that would be seen in the myth genre.	Life cycle of a plant is somewhat not clear in the myth genre.	Life cycle of a plant is vague.	Life cycle of a plant is not addressed.
Conventions	Demonstrates superior command of the conventions of the English language, with no errors in grammar, spelling, or usage.	Demonstrates command of the conventions of the English language, with no more than one error in grammar, spelling, or usage.	Demonstrates command of the conventions of the English language, with no more than two errors in grammar, spelling, or usage.	Demonstrates command of the conventions of the English language, with no more than three errors in grammar, spelling, or usage.	Demonstrates novice command of the conventions of the English language, with more than three errors in grammar, spelling, or usage.
					________ / 16

LESSON 3.2

Shoot for the Moon

Common Core State Standards

- RI.3.1
- RI.3.2
- RI.3.3
- RI.3.5
- RI.3.6
- RI.3.7
- RI.3.9
- RI.3.10
- RF.3.3
- RF.3.4
- W.3.1
- W.3.4
- W.3.5
- W.3.7
- W.3.10
- SL.3.1
- SL.3.2
- SL.3.3
- SL.3.4
- SL.3.6
- L.3.1
- L.3.2
- L.3.3
- L.3.4

Materials

- Lesson 3.2 Space Exploration
- Lesson 3.2 Preparing for Debate
- Lesson 3.2 Lincoln-Douglas Debate Format
- Lesson 3.2 Rubric: Self-Evaluation Debate
- Computer and Internet access
- Books and other resources to help students prepare for the debate
- Student copies of *Moonshot: The Flight of Apollo 11* by Brian Floca (read aloud; https://www.youtube.com/watch?v=LAo8JdPPKeE)
- Student copies of "A New Martian Machine" by Cameron Keady and Jeffrey Kluger (http://kidsahead.com/external/article/1058)
- Teacher's resources:
  - "Welcome to Debate" (http://www.saskdebate.com/media/3101/grab%20and%20go%20debate%20unit.pdf)
  - "Stage a Debate: A Primer for Teachers (Lincoln-Douglas Debate Format)" (http://www.educationworld.com/a_lesson/03/lp304-01.shtml)

Estimated Time

- 160 minutes

Objectives

In this lesson, students will:

- compare and contrast the most important points and key details presented on two nonfiction texts with related topics,
- determine personal position statement to a posed question, and
- debate with classmates.

Content

Students will analyze *Moonshot: The Flight of Apollo 11* by Brian Floca to determine the main idea and importance in a series of historical events. Students will then read an article about a more recent space mission. Students will compare and contrast the ideas presented in the two texts. Afterward, students research and develop a position regarding a debate statement. Students will then hold a debate to showcase their knowledge and opinions.

Prior Knowledge

Students will need to have some experience with the Lincoln-Douglas form of debate. Student knowledge in the history of space missions may enhance interest and prior knowledge for the content of the debate, but is not necessary for the lesson.

INSTRUCTIONAL SEQUENCE

1. Have students quickly jot down their knowledge of space and space travel, then share with the class.
2. Have students read *Moonshot: The Flight of Apollo 11* by Brian Floca and the article "A New Martian Machine" by Cameron Keady and Jeffrey Kluger. They should analyze the texts with partners or in small groups using Lesson 3.2 Space Exploration.
3. As students work, walk around to facilitate discussions when needed and provide help to any struggling students. You may wish to insert alternative articles or allow students to research their own questions about space travel.
4. After students complete the handout, explain that they will now prepare for a debate on a topic regarding space exploration. Read the position statement to students: *Space exploration is costly and takes much time and planning. Do you believe that it is worth using our country's resources to continue with space exploration?*
5. Explain that students will divide into two teams and take opposite sides of the issue. They will have access to books and the Internet in order to do additional research if needed. To prepare, students should use Lesson 3.2 Preparing for Debate and Lesson 3.2 Lincoln-Douglas Debate Format. Allow students to draw from a hat to determine which position they will take in the debate. One of the students can be the moderator or you may play that role yourself.

Teacher's Note. For more information on Lincoln-Douglas style debates, follow the steps below. You can also visit either of the sites listed under teacher resources in the Materials section.

- Begin by introducing the topic to students.
- Allow time for students to conduct additional research in order to increase their knowledge about the topic.
- Using notes taken during research, students should brainstorm possible debate points to support point of view of the team.
- Allow students time to practice for debate with team members.
- Hold the debate.

6. As students research additional information, help them organize facts they have learned about the topic into possible points to support their side of the issue.
7. Allow students time to practice within their group in order to get comfortable with the debate format and using evidence statements to support their point of view.
8. Have students use Lesson 3.2: Self-Evaluation Debate Rubric to evaluate their work during the debate.
9. Hold the debate. You may want to invite another class to attend. Have the class complete an exit ticket at the end of the debate stating which position they would take after hearing the arguments. Share the results with the students.

Extension Activities

Students may:

- write an informational essay explaining the advantages and disadvantages of space travel,
- create a poster or public service advertisement supporting his or her point of view on the lesson debate question in lieu of participating in the debate, or
- research any questions that may have arisen during the reading of the two articles and put their research findings in a visual report of some style.

NAME:______________________________ DATE:______________

LESSON 3.2

Space Exploration

Directions: Read the nonfiction text provided and discuss the text with your partner. Then work with your partner to answer the questions on this sheet to the best of your ability, using text evidence to support your claims.

1. What would you consider to be the main idea of *Moonshot: The Flight of Apollo 11* by Brian Floca? Use details from the text to support your answer.

2. What would you consider to be the main idea of the web article? Use details from the text to support your answer.

3. Complete the Venn diagram below to compare and contrast how the idea of space exploration is treated similarly and differently in the two texts you read.

Text 1: ______________________ Text 2: ______________________

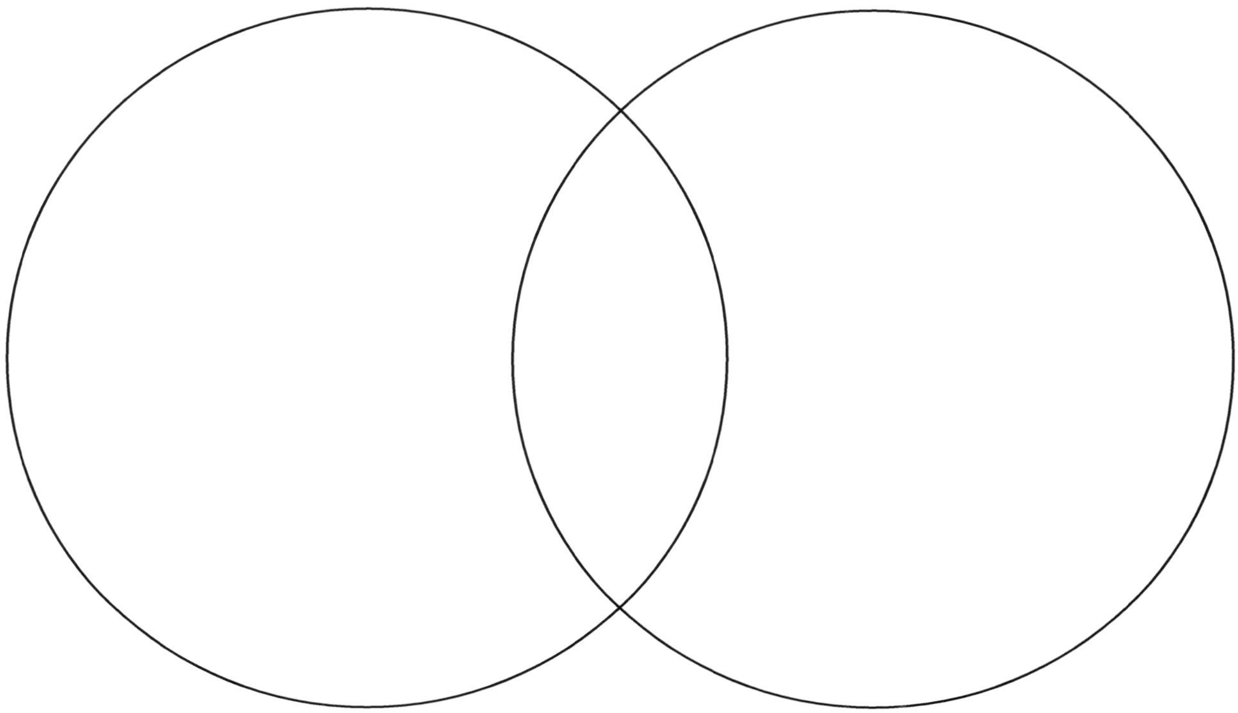

4. Explain how historical events, such as the flight of Apollo 11, led to future space travel and exploration, such as space exploration to other celestial bodies.

NAME:_______________ DATE:_______________

LESSON 3.2

Preparing for Debate

Directions: Using your side's position on the statement, research more about the topic of space exploration and flight. Use this handout to organize your thoughts.

Position: _______________

Research Notes		
Source	**Information Notes**	**How Can This Support My Position?**

Beliefs

Planning for the debate: Use the prompts below to help you gather your thoughts for the debate.

1. List three statements you will use to argue in support of your position.

2. How could your opposition rebut your statements above?

3. What would you say in return for your opposition's rebuts?

4. List two statements that the opposition may use to support their position.

5. How will you rebut those statements?

NAME:_______________ DATE:_______________

LESSON 3.2

Lincoln-Douglas Debate Format

Directions: Use the outline below to help you plan your debate.

1. Make opening remarks (briefly state your viewpoint and reasons to support your viewpoint).
2. Debate points to support your side of the issue. You will need at least three strong points.
3. Plan questions for your opposition.
4. Make closing remarks (briefly restate your viewpoint and reasons to support your viewpoint).

Choose team members' roles:

1. **Lead debater(s):** States the opening remarks.
2. **Questioner(s)/cross examiner(s):** Poses questions to the opposition.
3. **Question responder(s):** Answers questions from the opposition.
4. **Rebutter(s):** Offers the rebuttal statement(s).
5. **Summarizer(s):** States the closing remarks.

Familiarize yourself with the outline for the structure of the debate in order to better prepare for the actual event. Practice with teammates, having people play the role of the opposition.

1. Affirmative debater presents opening remarks.
2. Affirmative debater presents evidence to support affirmative side of the issue.
3. Negative debater asks any questions for the affirmative debater.
4. Negative debater presents opening remarks.
5. Negative debater presents evidence to support negative side of the issue.
6. Affirmative debater asks any questions for the negative debater.
7. Affirmative debater offers rebuttal.
8. Negative debater offers rebuttal.
9. Affirmative debater offers closing remarks.
10. Negative debater offers closing remarks.

NAME:______________________________ DATE:______________

LESSON 3.2 RUBRIC

Self-Evaluation Debate

	Exceeds Expectations 5 points	Proficient 4 points	Developed 3 points	Emerging 2 points	Novice 1 point
Preparation for Debate	I took on the task of supporting my side without hesitation or complaint. I used my time efficiently and looked for multiple outside sources to support my side.	I took on the task of supporting my side without hesitation or complaint. I used my time efficiently to help to support my side.	I took on the task of supporting my side. I used my time efficiently to support my side.	I took on the task of supporting my side, but with some hesitation.	I worked with my debate team, but did not really contribute to researching or supporting my team in many ways.
During Debate	I worked to support my side with clarity and facts gained from research. I was respectful in all exchanges during the debate and followed the appropriate debate format.	I worked to support my side with facts gained from research. I was respectful in all exchanges during the debate and followed the appropriate debate format.	I worked to support my side with facts gained from research. I followed the appropriate debate format.	I worked to support my side with facts gained from research. I may have strayed from the appropriate debate format.	I strayed from facts or may have not followed the appropriate debate format.
Speaking and Listening	I spoke loudly, clearly, and to my audience and the opposing team during the debate. I also showed evidence of truly listening by making adjustments to my points according to the opposition's statements.	I spoke loudly, clearly, and to the opposing team during the debate. I also showed evidence of truly listening by making adjustments to my points according to the opposition's statements.	I spoke loudly, clearly, and to the opposing team during the debate. I listened to the opposition's statements, but did not make any adjustments to my points based on the statements.	My speech was hard to hear due to clarity or volume. I showed evidence of truly listening by making adjustments to my points according to the opposition's statements.	My speech was hard to hear due to clarity or volume. I did not show much evidence of truly listening to the opposition's points.
					________ / 12

LESSON 3.3

Believe in Yourself

Common Core State Standards

- RL.3.1
- RL.3.2
- RL.3.6
- W.3.2
- W.3.4
- W.3.10
- SL.3.1
- SL.3.2
- SL.3.6
- L.3.1
- L.3.2
- L.3.3
- L.3.4

Materials

- Lesson 3.3 Dr. Martin Luther King, Jr.'s Speech
- Lesson 3.3 Literature Analysis Model
- Lesson 3.3 The Power of Poetry
- Lesson 3.3 Representing My Beliefs
- Student copies of "Your World" by Georgia Douglas Johnson
- Student copies of "Try, Try Again" by T. H. Palmer
- Video: "I Have a Dream" speech by Dr. Martin Luther King, Jr. (available online)
- Transcript of "I Have a Dream" speech by Dr. Martin Luther King, Jr. (optional; http://www.archives.gov/press/exhibits/dream-speech.pdf)

Estimated Time

- 110 minutes

Teacher's Note. The Lexile level for "I Have a Dream" is very high and more suitable for highly advanced readers. If you wish to use this with average third-grade readers, you will need to edit the speech to make it more Lexile friendly.

Objectives

In this lesson, students will:

- determine the central message of poems, and
- create a symbolic representation of a strong personal belief.

Content

Students will consider their thoughts on beliefs by watching an archival video of a portion of Dr. Martin Luther King, Jr.'s "I Have a Dream" speech. Students will then read "Your World" by Georgia Douglas Johnson and "Try, Try Again" by T. H. Palmer to analyze what each speaker says about the concept of belief. Students will then synthesize the knowledge gained from the poetry and archival video to determine a strong personal belief of their own and represent it in a symbolic manner.

Prior Knowledge

Students will need to be familiar with poetry terminology, such as *line* and *stanza*. Students would also benefit from experience identifying figurative language devices in poetry to gain a better understanding of the poem. Students will need to be able to identify from which point of view a piece of writing is written.

INSTRUCTIONAL SEQUENCE

1. Ask students: *How have you come to change any preconceptions you had about beliefs since our unit has begun?* Allow students time to think and then discuss with peers. Students may wish to write down a few notes comparing their thoughts then and now.
2. Explain to students that they will read two poems about literature and watch a primary source archival video of a famous speech to further develop their ideas about belief.
3. In the video, Dr. Martin Luther King, Jr. addresses a crowd during the famous March on Washington. As they watch, students should use Lesson 3.3 Dr. Martin Luther King, Jr.'s Speech to organize their thoughts about:
   - words or phrases King uses that emphasize and support his central message or beliefs,
   - facial expressions and body language that help support King's strong beliefs, and
   - how they think the people feel about King's beliefs.

4. Facilitate a whole-class discussion after the video about students' thoughts. Students should take notes during the discussion to use for their final project in this lesson.
5. Allow students to work with a partner to read and analyze "Your World" and "Try, Try Again." For an initial analysis, work with students to complete Lesson 3.3 Literature Analysis Model (about one or both poems) after an initial close read. (See pp. 3–4 for additional information about using the Literature Analysis Model.)
6. Distribute Lesson 3.3 The Power of Poetry. Give students time to work on the questions. Once students have finished discussing poems with their partners, facilitate a whole-class discussion to review their thoughts.
7. Explain that they will use their ideas about belief gained from the two poems and the archival video to create a symbolic representation (e.g., collage, drawing) of an issue in which they strongly believe (e.g., the belief in freedom to express oneself, belief in a religious figure). Have students use Lesson 3.3 Representing My Beliefs to brainstorm their ideas before developing the visual representation.
8. Allow students to share their symbolic representation with their peers.

Extension Activities

Students may:

- create their own poem about a belief they have, or
- create a musical score for their essay or for King's speech and present it to the class.

NAME:____ DATE:________________

LESSON 3.3

Dr. Martin Luther King, Jr.'s Speech

Directions: Use the chart below to help organize your thoughts when watching Dr. King's speech during the March on Washington, looking for elements he used that support the main idea of belief.

Words/Phrases

Repetition

Facial Expressions

Other Elements I Noticed

NAME: ______________________ DATE: ______________

LESSON 3.3

Literature Analysis Model

Directions: Complete this Literature Analysis Model about the assigned poems.

	Chosen or Assigned Text: ______________
Key Words	
Important Ideas	
Tone	
Mood	
Imagery	
Symbolism	
Structure of Writing	

Note. Adapted from *Exploring America in the 1950s* (p. 10) by M. Sandling & K. L. Chandler, 2014, Waco, TX: Prufrock Press. Copyright 2014 by Center for Gifted Education. Adapted with permission.

NAME:______________________________ DATE:______________

LESSON 3.3
The Power of Poetry

Directions: Read the poems "Your World" by Georgia Douglas Johnson and "Try, Try, Again" by T. H. Palmer with your partner. As you read, discuss any sections of the poems that are unclear. Then answer the questions below.

"Your World"

1. How would you describe the speaker in the poem? Use text evidence to support your thoughts.

2. How does the speaker's tone affect the mood of this poem?

3. How does the second stanza build on the first? What does this tell you about the change in the belief of the speaker?

4. What is the message the speaker of this poem wants to share with the reader?

"Try, Try Again"

1. What is the central message of this poem? Based on text evidence, why do you think this?

2. Based on the thoughts expressed in this poem, what do you think the speaker's belief would be regarding what one should do when encountering obstacles?

3. How do the speaker's beliefs in this poem compare and contrast with that of the narrator in "Your World"? Dr. King in his speech? You own personal beliefs?

NAME:______________________________ DATE:______________

LESSON 3.3

Representing My Beliefs

Directions: Complete the chart below to help you brainstorm ideas for your visual representation.

My Belief	Pictures or Images to Represent It	Possible Symbolic Representation Format
Belief in freedom of expression	*American flag*	*Collage of photos of pictures of the American flag*

Beliefs

LESSON 3.4

People Hold Beliefs

Common Core State Standards

- RL.3.1
- RL.3.2
- RL.3.3
- W.3.3
- W.3.4
- W.3.10
- SL.3.1
- SL.3.2
- SL.3.6
- L.3.1
- L.3.2
- L.3.3
- L.3.4
- L.3.5
- L.3.6

Materials

- Lesson 3.4 Examining for Beliefs
- Lesson 3.4 Characters Make the News
- Lesson 3.4 Rubric: Characters Make the News
- Student copies of *Charlotte's Web* by E. B. White or excerpt of *Charlotte's Web* found in the CCSS Appendix B (http://corestandards.org/assets/Appendix_B.pdf)
- Student copies of newspaper articles/editorials (at least three per student)

Estimated Time

- 90 minutes

> ***Teacher's Note.*** The newspaper articles should be appropriate for your school community and if possible reflect an area being studied in one of the other subjects to make a crosscurricular connection.

Objectives

In this lesson, students will:

- analyze fictional literature and nonfiction texts,
- determine the point of view of a certain author or character, and
- compose an original newspaper article or editorial to reflect the beliefs of a specific literary character.

Content

With a small group, students will discuss and write a response to a tiered question regarding the belief of a character in E. B. White's *Charlotte's Web.* Students will then examine newspaper editorials to see how people's beliefs show through in their writing. After examining newspaper articles and editorials, students will create their own newspaper article or editorial that reflects the belief of a character in E. B. White's *Charlotte's Web.*

Prior Knowledge

Students will need to have read or heard *Charlotte's Web* by E. B. White. Students should also be familiar with the organization and format of newspaper editorials.

INSTRUCTIONAL SEQUENCE

1. Have students read the excerpt of E. B. White's *Charlotte's Web* in small groups.
2. Have each group discuss a question listed below (answers will vary). You may allow the students to choose their own questions or assign questions based on ability.
   - **Tier I:** What evidence from the text shows that Fern values animals' lives? How do you know? Use examples from the text to support your thoughts. (Students may include when Fern cries to save Wilbur, how Fern treats Wilbur as a baby, and so forth.)
   - **Tier II:** What beliefs does Fern have concerning animals' lives? Use examples from the text to support your thoughts. (Students may notice that Fern values animals' lives because she is persistent in her mission to save Wilbur.)
   - **Tier III:** Fern begs her father not to kill Wilbur. How does this prove that Fern truly values animals' lives? Use examples from the text to support your thoughts. (Students may mention that Fern must value animals' lives because she continued to ask until she was finally granted her wish to keep Wilbur.)

Allow students time to discuss their thoughts on their question, referring to the text for support.

3. After students have shared their written responses, explain that just as characters in fictional literature have beliefs, so do people in the real world. Many times, the author's message is evident in his or her writing. Students will now examine newspaper articles and editorials to find evidence of the author's beliefs in the writing. Have students use Lesson 3.4 Examining for Beliefs to guide their thoughts.
4. Afterward, explain that they will look back at *Charlotte's Web* and the beliefs of some other characters in the novel. Students will create a newspaper editorial or article outlining the beliefs of another character from his or her point of view. Students will address one of the scenarios listed on Lesson 3.4 Characters Make the News. Students will need to use Lesson 3.4 Rubric: Characters Make the News to guide their writing.
5. Display all student editorials or articles to be viewed by other students.

Extension Activities

Students may:

- create a news report for a TV show using their article as a basis for their show, or
- interview a local newspaper reporter or editor about his or her writing process and how his or her beliefs help to shape this process.

NAME:______________________________ DATE:______________

LESSON 3.4

Examining for Beliefs

Directions: Use the questions below to guide your analysis of the newspaper articles provided.

1. What is the main idea of each newspaper article or editorial?

2. How might the main idea be important to the author(s) of the article or editorial?

3. How does the author(s) use language for effect to show shades of meaning?

4. How might language help to support an author's beliefs?

NAME:____________________ DATE:__________

LESSON 3.4

Characters Make the News

Directions: Choose a character from *Charlotte's Web* who is listed below. Write a newspaper editorial from the point of view of this character to show his or her beliefs, based on what you know about the character from your reading. Then choose a scenario from the list below to address in your editorial. Use Lesson 3.4 Rubric: Characters Make the News to guide your writing.

Characters

1. Charlotte
2. Wilbur
3. Mr. Zuckerman
4. Templeton

Scenarios

1. Wilbur will be kept forever as a pet pig.
2. A memorial will be held for Charlotte's life.
3. Templeton's contributions helped save Wilbur's life.
4. Fern saves Wilbur and keeps him as a pet.
5. Mr. Zuckerman's farm is being sold to another owner.

NAME:______________________________ DATE:______________

LESSON 3.4 RUBRIC

Characters Make the News

	Exceeds Expectations 5 points	Proficient 4 points	Developed 3 points	Emerging 2 points	Novice 1 point
Point of View	Written from the point of view of one of the characters from *Charlotte's Web*, using unique words and phrases that are common to the character.	Written from the point of view of one of the characters from *Charlotte's Web*, using words and phrases that are common to the character.	Written from the point of view of one of the characters from *Charlotte's Web*.	Written from a character's perspective, but it is not clear which character.	Does not seem to be written by any of the characters in *Charlotte's Web*.
Scenario Content	Written within one of the scenarios, with much elaboration and detail given to the scenario.	Written within one of the scenarios, with much detail given to the scenario.	Written within one of the scenarios.	Written within one of the scenarios, but strays off topic several times during the editorial.	Not written to address one of the scenarios.
Text Evidence	Uses at least five examples to support the scenario.	Uses four examples to support the scenario.	Uses three examples to support the scenario.	Uses two examples to support the scenario.	Uses one or no examples to support the scenario.
Conventions	Demonstrates superior command of the conventions of the English language, with no errors in grammar, spelling, or usage.	Demonstrates command of the conventions of the English language, with no more than one error in grammar, spelling, or usage.	Demonstrates command of the conventions of the English language, with no more than two errors in grammar, spelling, or usage.	Demonstrates command of the conventions of the English language, with no more than three errors in grammar, spelling, or usage.	Demonstrates novice command of the conventions of the English language, with more than three errors in grammar, spelling, or usage.
					______ / 16

NAME:______________________ DATE:______________

Beliefs

UNIT III

Culminating Essay Prompt

Directions: In this unit, you read about beliefs and how people express them. Thinking about the visual representation you created in the third lesson of this unit, write an essay explaining why you have that belief. Include information about factors and people that have influenced you to believe that way.

UNIT IV

Perseverance

This unit centers on the ideas related to perseverance as shown by characters, both fictional and historical. Within the unit, students will read, analyze, evaluate, and interpret poetry, novels, and nonfiction texts with themes related to perseverance and how a character's traits, an author's point of view, or a historical figure's personal character related to this theme. They will consider the obstacles faced by various fictional and historical characters and examine how each persevered through adversity to achieve goals and dreams. Students will demonstrate their understanding of the concept of perseverance through various projects, narrative writing, informational writing, persuasive writing, and poetry.

LESSON 4.1

The Importance of Perseverance

Common Core State Standards

- RL.3.1
- RL.3.2
- RL.3.3
- RL.3.6
- W.3.1
- W.3.10
- SL.3.1
- SL.3.2
- SL.3.6
- L.3.1
- L.3.2
- L.3.3
- L.3.4

Materials

- Lesson 4.1 Character Perseverance
- Lesson 4.1 Character Perseverance Flyer
- Lesson 4.1 Rubric: Character Perseverance Flyer
- Student copies of *The Search for Delicious* by Natalie Babbitt
- Student copies of *The Phantom Tollbooth* by Norton Juster, *The Neverending Story* by Michael Ende, or *The One-Eyed Giant* by Mary Pope Osborne (optional)
- Materials to develop a flyer

Estimated Time

- 90 minutes

Objectives

In this lesson, students will:

- analyze fictional literature to determine the central message of stories, and
- compose a persuasive essay explaining a position of a certain topic.

Content

Students will analyze a novel, *The Search for Delicious*, to determine how the protagonist perseveres through many obstacles. Students will use their knowledge of perseverance to create an original advertisement, which will persuade teachers to purchase the novel because it showcases the power of perseverance.

Prior Knowledge

Students will need to have read *The Search for Delicious* by Natalie Babbitt (or one of the alternative texts suggested). Students will need to be able to identify and analyze the protagonist of a piece of fictional literature.

INSTRUCTIONAL SEQUENCE

1. Ask students to turn to a partner and briefly discuss how they thought the protagonist in the novel handled challenging situations. Encourage students to think about positives and negatives of the character's abilities to handle challenges, as well as aspects of the character's personality that caused him to act as he did throughout the novel.
2. Students will use their knowledge from reading *The Search for Delicious* to answer the questions on Lesson 4.1 Character Perseverance. Students may work in small groups.
3. Discuss the idea of *perseverance*. Guiding questions may include:
   - Does the story remind you of anything that ever happened to you?
   - What does *perseverance* mean to you?
   - What is an example of a time when you have had to persevere through an obstacle?
   - If it was difficult, how did you feel? Were you able to do it? Who or what helped you? Who or what didn't help you?
   - How did you work through problems to overcome the obstacles you were facing?
   - How did you feel after you persevered and were able to resolve the problems?

4. With partners, have students complete a flyer outlining how their character persevered through challenges throughout the novel. Distribute Lesson 4.1 Character Perseverance Flyer. Read the following scenario to the students:

   A book publisher wants to make a flyer explaining how the novel you read would be good for teachers to help show students how characters persevere through obstacles. The publisher is hoping that teachers will buy this book if they see how clearly the character overcomes challenges and how they can share this with students. Create a flyer that the book publisher could give to teachers. Be sure that your flyer clearly states:
   - the title of your book,
   - the main character,
   - the problem the main character encountered, and
   - how the main character overcame or persevered through the challenges.

5. Have students use Lesson 4.1 Rubric: Character Perseverance Flyer to make sure they include the necessary information on their flyer.
6. Allow students to share their flyers or display them around the room to be viewed.

Extension Activity

Students may make a poster from the character's point of view encouraging others to persevere through tough obstacles.

NAME:________________________________ DATE:______________

LESSON 4.1
Character Perseverance

Directions: Complete the character trait web below using Gaylen's examples of perseverance as seen in the text. Be sure to provide page numbers for where you are finding your text evidence.

GAYLEN'S EXAMPLES OF PERSEVERANCE

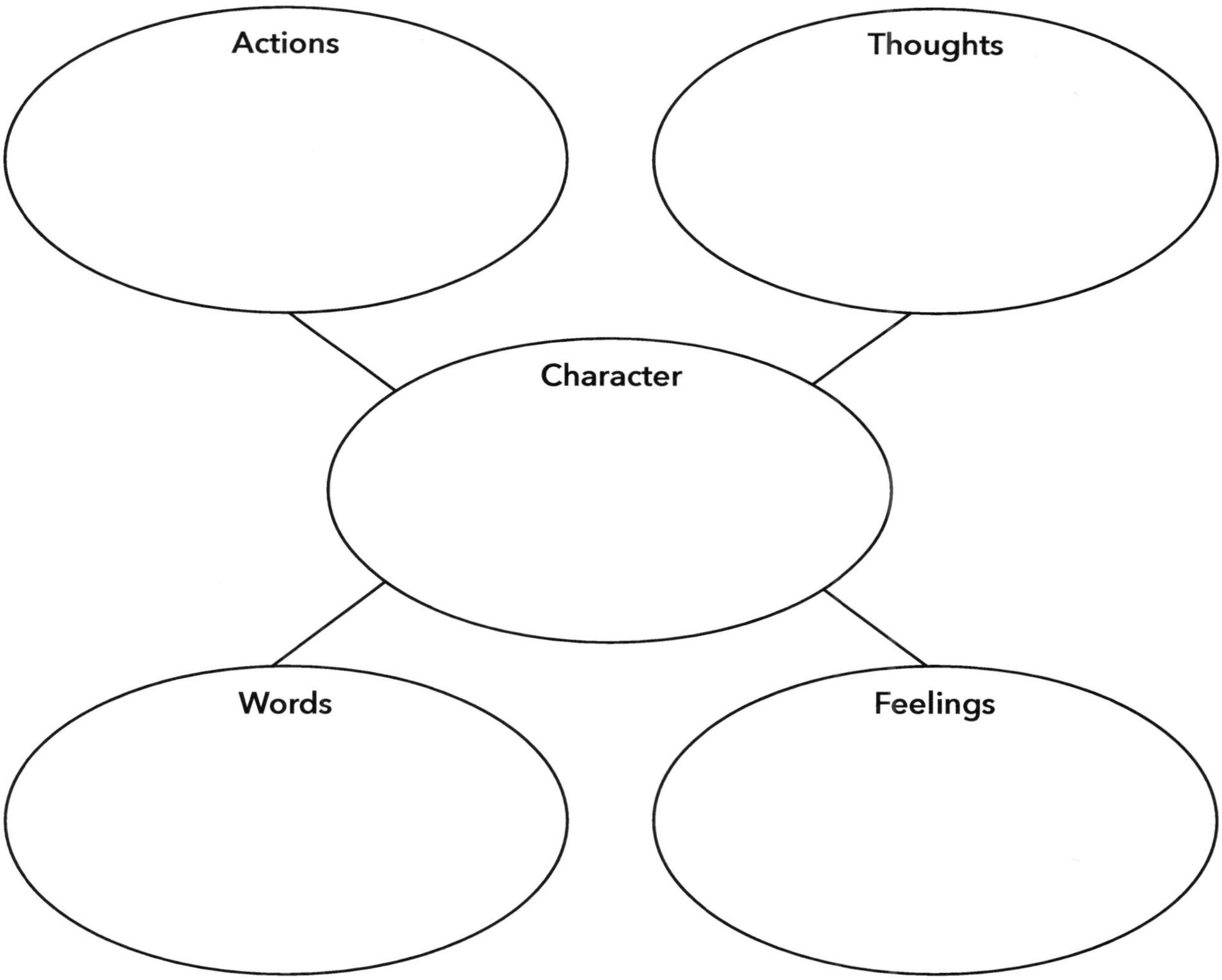

Discuss the following questions with your group members, using your text to support your thoughts. Then, answer the questions below using your knowledge gained from the group discussion.

1. How would you describe the protagonist in this book? Why?

2. Explain how the protagonist worked to solve the problems in order to overcome the obstacles.

3. How does the protagonist's character traits show the central message of perseverance?

4. If you were the character in the story going through the same challenges, how would you have persevered? Would you have made any different decisions from those of the character?

5. How can reading this novel help inspire readers to persevere in their lives? Use examples from the text to support your thoughts.

NAME:______________________________ DATE:______________

LESSON 4.1

Character Perseverance Flyer

Directions: A book publisher wants to make a flyer explaining how the novel you read would be good for teachers to use to help show students how characters persevere through obstacles. The publisher is hoping that teachers will buy this book if they see how clearly the character overcomes challenges and how they can share this with students. Create a flyer that the book publisher could give to teachers.

Be sure that your flyer:

1. clearly states the title of your book,
2. clearly states the main character,
3. clearly states the problem the main character encountered, and
4. clearly states how the main character overcame or persevered through the challenges.

Perseverance

NAME:______________________ DATE:______________

LESSON 4.1 RUBRIC

Character Perseverance Flyer

	Exceeds Expectations 5 points	Proficient 4 points	Developed 3 points	Emerging 2 points	Novice 1 point
Title and Main Character	Clearly states the title and main character in a unique display that is attractive to the audience.	Clearly states the title and main character in a display that is attractive to the audience.	Clearly states the title and main character.	Missing either the title or the main character.	Missing both the title and the main character.
Main Problem	Clearly states the main problem in his or her own words and accurately expresses the major conflict of the novel.	Clearly states the main problem in his or her own words and accurately expresses the one of the conflicts of the novel.	Clearly states the main problem, but not in his or her own words, and accurately expresses the major conflict of the novel.	Clearly states the main problem but not in his or her own words, and accurately expresses one of the conflicts of the novel.	Does not clearly state the main problem anywhere.
Perseverance	Clearly states how the novel would be good for helping students learn to persevere through at least two text examples written in their own words.	Clearly states how the novel would be good for helping students learn to persevere through a text example written in their own words.	Vaguely states how the novel would be good for helping students learn to persevere through at least two text examples written in their own words.	Vaguely states how the novel would be good for helping students learn to persevere through at least two text examples.	Vaguely states how the novel would be good for helping students learn to persevere through one text example.
Conventions	Demonstrates superior command of the conventions of the English language, with no errors in grammar, spelling, or usage.	Demonstrates command of the conventions of the English language, with no more than one error in grammar, spelling, or usage.	Demonstrates command of the conventions of the English language, with no more than two errors in grammar, spelling, or usage.	Demonstrates command of the conventions of the English language, with no more than three errors in grammar, spelling, or usage.	Demonstrates novice command of the conventions of the English language, with more than three errors in grammar, spelling, or usage.
					________ / 16

LESSON 4.2

The Power of Perseverance

Common Core State Standards

- RL.3.1
- RL.3.2
- RL.3.3
- RL3.4
- RL.3.6
- RL.3.7
- RL.3.10
- W.3.3
- W.3.10
- SL.3.1
- SL.3.2
- SL.3.6
- L.3.1
- L.3.2
- L.3.3
- L.3.4

Materials

- Lesson 4.2 Literature Analysis Model
- Lesson 4.2 Developing the Central Message
- Lesson 4.2 Rubric: Perseverance Diary Entry
- *My Father's Dragon* by Ruth Stiles Gannett (http://digital.library.upenn.edu/women/gannett/dragon/dragon.html)
- Sticky notes

Estimated Time

- 110 minutes

Objectives

In this lesson, students will:

- analyze fictional literature to determine the central message, and
- compose a diary entry from the point of view of a fictional character.

Content

Students will analyze the novel, *My Father's Dragon*, in order to determine the central message, as evidenced by the main character's thoughts, words, feelings, and actions. Students will then write a diary entry from the point of view of Elmer stating how he persevered through the challenges he faced to free the dragon.

Prior Knowledge

Students will need to have read *My Father's Dragon* by Ruth Stiles Gannett. Students will need experience using characters' thoughts, words, feelings, and actions to support the central message of a story.

INSTRUCTIONAL SEQUENCE

1. For an initial analysis of the novel, work with students to complete Lesson 4.2 Literature Analysis Model (preferably about one chapter that most exemplifies the idea of *perseverance*) after they have done an initial close read. Consider emphasizing specific boxes that will be the focus of this lesson. (See pp. 3–4 for additional information about using the Literature Analysis Model.)
2. (Optional) Have students annotate a chapter of the book that best exemplifies the idea of *perseverance*. Each student will need a printed copy or an electronic version, as long as they will be able to annotate the text. Students may use sticky notes for annotation if writing on or electronically highlighting the text is not possible. Have students use the following procedure:
   - read the story carefully,
   - identify the characters (circle), and
   - identify clue words for the central message (underline).
3. Divide students into groups of 3–4. Explain to students that they will be analyzing *My Father's Dragon* to determine how the author used the main character's thoughts, feelings, words, and actions to develop the central message of the story.
4. Distribute Lesson 4.2 Developing the Central Message and explain that students will use the graphic organizer to help guide their discussion about the text. Allow students time to work on questions, while circulating to facilitate discussions and clarify understanding.
5. Afterward, have students compose their diary entry from the point of view of Elmer. In the diary entry, students should use Elmer's voice to explain how he made the choices to persevere through the obstacles in order to free the baby dragon. Distribute Lesson 4.2 Rubric: Perseverance Diary Entry so students can reference that as they write.
6. Allow students to share their diary entry with a partner or with the class.

Extension Activities

Students may:

- create a story map of how the dragon became a prisoner on the island,
- create a brochure for tourists who might want to tour the island in the story, or
- write a more detailed diary entry for each obstacle Elmer faced during his adventure and put the entries together in a class book or "Diary of Elmer."

NAME:______________________________ DATE:______________

LESSON 4.2

Literature Analysis Model

Directions: Complete this Literature Analysis Model about *My Father's Dragon* by Ruth Stiles Gannett.

	My Father's Dragon **by Ruth Stiles Gannett**
Key Words	
Important Ideas	
Tone	
Mood	
Imagery	
Symbolism	
Structure of Writing	

Note. Adapted from *Exploring America in the 1950s* (p. 10) by M. Sandling & K. L. Chandler, 2014, Waco, TX: Prufrock Press. Copyright 2014 by Center for Gifted Education. Adapted with permission.

Perseverance

NAME:______________________________ DATE:______________

LESSON 4.2

Developing the Central Message

Directions: Use evidence from the text to complete the web in order to help you gather your thoughts about the central message of *My Father's Dragon*. You will then use your thoughts to compose a diary entry from the point of view of Elmer describing how his choices during his adventure showed the theme of perseverance.

Thoughts

Words

Actions

Feelings

How do Elmer's thoughts, words, actions, and feelings help lead to the central message of perseverance?

NAME:______________________________ DATE:______________

LESSON 4.2 RUBRIC

Perseverance Diary Entry

	Exceeds Expectations 5 points	Proficient 4 points	Developed 3 points	Emerging 2 points	Novice 1 point
Point of View	Told from Elmer's point of view; written in a manner that is similar to his thoughts, words, actions, and feelings displayed in the text; displays student's originality.	Told from Elmer's point of view; written in a manner that is similar to his thoughts, words, actions, and feelings displayed in the text.	Told from Elmer's point of view; supported by similarities in thoughts, words, actions, or feelings displayed in the text.	Told from Elmer's point of view; does not display any similarities to the thoughts, words, actions, or feelings displayed in the mentor text.	Not told from Elmer's point of view.
Perseverance	Clearly states ways in which Elmer shows the trait of perseverance through at least four examples from the text.	Clearly states ways in which Elmer shows the trait of perseverance through three examples from the text.	Clearly states ways in which Elmer shows the trait of perseverance through two examples from the text.	Clearly states ways in which Elmer shows the trait of perseverance through an example from the text.	Does not use any examples from the text to support how Elmer showed the trait of perseverance.
Conventions	Demonstrates superior command of the conventions of the English language, with no errors in grammar, spelling, or usage.	Demonstrates command of the conventions of the English language, with no more than one error in grammar, spelling, or usage.	Demonstrates command of the conventions of the English language, with no more than two errors in grammar, spelling, or usage.	Demonstrates command of the conventions of the English language, with no more than three errors in grammar, spelling, or usage.	Demonstrates novice command of the conventions of the English language, with more than three errors in grammar, spelling, or usage.
					________ / 12

LESSON 4.3

Perseverance for a Cause

Common Core State Standards

- RI.3.1
- RI.3.2
- RI.3.3
- RI.3.4
- RI.3.6
- RI.3.7
- RI.3.10
- W.3.3
- W.3.10
- SL.3.1
- SL.3.2
- SL.3.6
- L.3.1
- L.3.2
- L.3.3
- L.3.4

Materials

- Lesson 4.3 Persevere for a Cause
- Video: *Martin Luther King and the March on Washington* by Frances E. Ruffin (http://www.watchknowlearn.org/Video.aspx?VideoID=36289&CategoryID=10506)
- Sticky notes

Estimated Time

- 90 minutes

Objectives

In this lesson, students will:

- analyze nonfiction texts to determine point of view and how it affects the text, and
- compose an informational essay based on a conceptual question.

Content

Students will close read *Martin Luther King and the March on Washington* by Frances E. Ruffin. Then students will write an extended response using text evidence to a text-based conceptual question.

Prior Knowledge

Students will need experience determining the point of view of a text.

INSTRUCTIONAL SEQUENCE

1. Ask students how they would feel if they were planning to roller skate to the nation's capital to hear someone speak. Ask students whom they would consider important enough to see that they would complete this impressive journey. Explain that they are going to read a

book about how many people traveled all the way to Washington, DC, to hear Dr. Martin Luther King, Jr. give a speech.

2. With partners, have students read *Martin Luther King and the March on Washington* by Frances E. Ruffin.
3. (Optional) Have students annotate a chapter of the book that best exemplifies the idea of *perseverance*. Each student will need a printed copy or an electronic version, as long as they will be able to annotate the text. Students may use sticky notes for annotation if writing on or electronically highlighting the text is not possible. Have students use the following procedure:
   - read the text carefully,
   - identify the historical figures (circle), and
   - identify clue words for the main idea (underline).

4. Distribute Lesson 4.3 Persevere for a Cause. Allow students time to read the story and answer the questions, including the essay question (Extend Your Thinking). Walk around the room and assist anyone who may need clarification in terms of vocabulary or concepts.
5. Have students utilize peer and teacher comments on the completed essay to help revise and edit the essay for a final draft.
6. Allow students time to share their final draft with partners, as a whole-class presentation, or through a gallery walk.

Extension Activities

Students may:

- conduct additional research to offer several different viewpoints on this important historical event, or
- create a collage of examples of perseverance using images from the March on Washington.

NAME:______________________________ DATE:______________

LESSON 4.3

Persevere for a Cause

Directions: Work with a partner to discuss and answer the following questions after reading *Martin Luther King and the March on Washington* by Frances E. Ruffin.

1. What does the photograph of the man who roller-skated have to say about perseverance? How do photographs or illustrations help support the main idea of the text?

2. Dr. Martin Luther King, Jr. faced threats and imprisonment while fighting to gain equal civil rights for all Americans. How does this show perseverance?

3. What are some other actions taken by the people who participated in the March on Washington that demonstrate perseverance?

4. How did the perseverance of the people of the Civil Rights Movement lead to equal treatment of all Americans?

Extend Your Thinking

After reading *Martin Luther King and the March on Washington* by Frances E. Ruffin, how do you think many African Americans felt regarding the importance of persevering until all Americans were granted equal civil rights? Below, write an extended response essay to share your thoughts.

LESSON 4.4

Perseverance by Children

Common Core State Standards

- RI.3.1
- RI.3.4
- RI.3.5
- RI.3.6
- RI.3.9
- RI.3.10
- W.3.2
- W.3.10
- SL.3.1
- SL.3.2
- SL.3.6
- L.3.1
- L.3.2
- L.3.3

Materials

- Lesson 4.4 Character Trait Venn Diagram
- Lesson 4.4 Rubric: Traits of Perseverance
- Student copies of *The Story of Ruby Bridges* by Robert Coles
- Student copies of *Through My Eyes* by Ruby Bridges

Estimated Time

- 120 minutes

Objectives

In this lesson, students will:

- analyze historical figures based on researched gained through reading nonfiction texts,
- compare and contrast important points and key details presented in two texts on the same topic, and
- compose an informational essay regarding the characteristics of a historical figure.

Content

Students will answer a few questions to see that people, including themselves, have many layers that can motivate them to do many things, including persevering through hardships. Students will use what they know about Ruby Bridges from reading *The Story of Ruby Bridges* by Robert Coles and *Through My Eyes* by Ruby Bridges to develop an essay in which they support a certain point of view.

Prior Knowledge

Students will need to have read *The Story of Ruby Bridges* by Robert Coles and *Through My Eyes* by Ruby Bridges before beginning this lesson.

INSTRUCTIONAL SEQUENCE

1. Ask students to think about a situation in which they were required to show perseverance and share the example with a neighbor. Students may mention a time in which they had to problem-solve during a science experiment or when they had to continue to practice to get better at a sport.
2. Have the students discuss the following questions with each other:
   - Does the story remind you of anything that ever happened to you?
   - What does *perseverance* mean to you?
   - What is an example of a time when you have had to persevere through an obstacle?
   - If it was difficult, how did you feel? Were you able to do it? Who or what helped you? Who or what didn't help you?
   - How did you work through problems to overcome the obstacles you were facing?
   - How did you feel after you persevered and were able to resolve the problems?

3. Explain to students that just as they can gain information about a character from fictional texts, they can also gain information about real-life historical figures from texts. They are going to complete a character trait web for Ruby Bridges, using the two texts, *The Story of Ruby Bridges* by Robert Coles and *Through My Eyes* by Ruby Bridges, as well as information from their own lives.
4. Distribute Lesson 4.4 Character Trait Venn Diagram and allow students time to work independently or with a partner. Students should base their answers to the questions on their point of view, not from that of the narrator.
5. Afterward, students should compose a 3–5 paragraph essay that outlines character traits that help people persevere through challenges in life. Students need to be sure to support their answers with text evidence. Students should use Lesson 4.4 Rubric: Traits of Perseverance to help them compose their essays.

Teacher's Note. Alternative assessments may include having students create an infographic using a site such as Glogster, a PowerPoint or Prezi, or a poster to demonstrate their knowledge. The rubric can be adapted to fit the alternate form of assessment.

Extension Activities

Students may:

- create a song about what traits are needed in order to persevere through life challenges,
- debate the prompt using their essay as support, or
- interview an adult in their lives who demonstrates some character traits similar to Ruby Bridges that have helped them to persevere through challenges. Allow students to record answers in the style of a newspaper or magazine article and share with the class.

NAME:____ DATE:______________

LESSON 4.4

Character Trait Venn Diagram

Directions: Use the Venn diagram below to list some of the character traits demonstrated by Ruby Bridges in both texts that show perseverance compared to some of your own character traits that show perseverance.

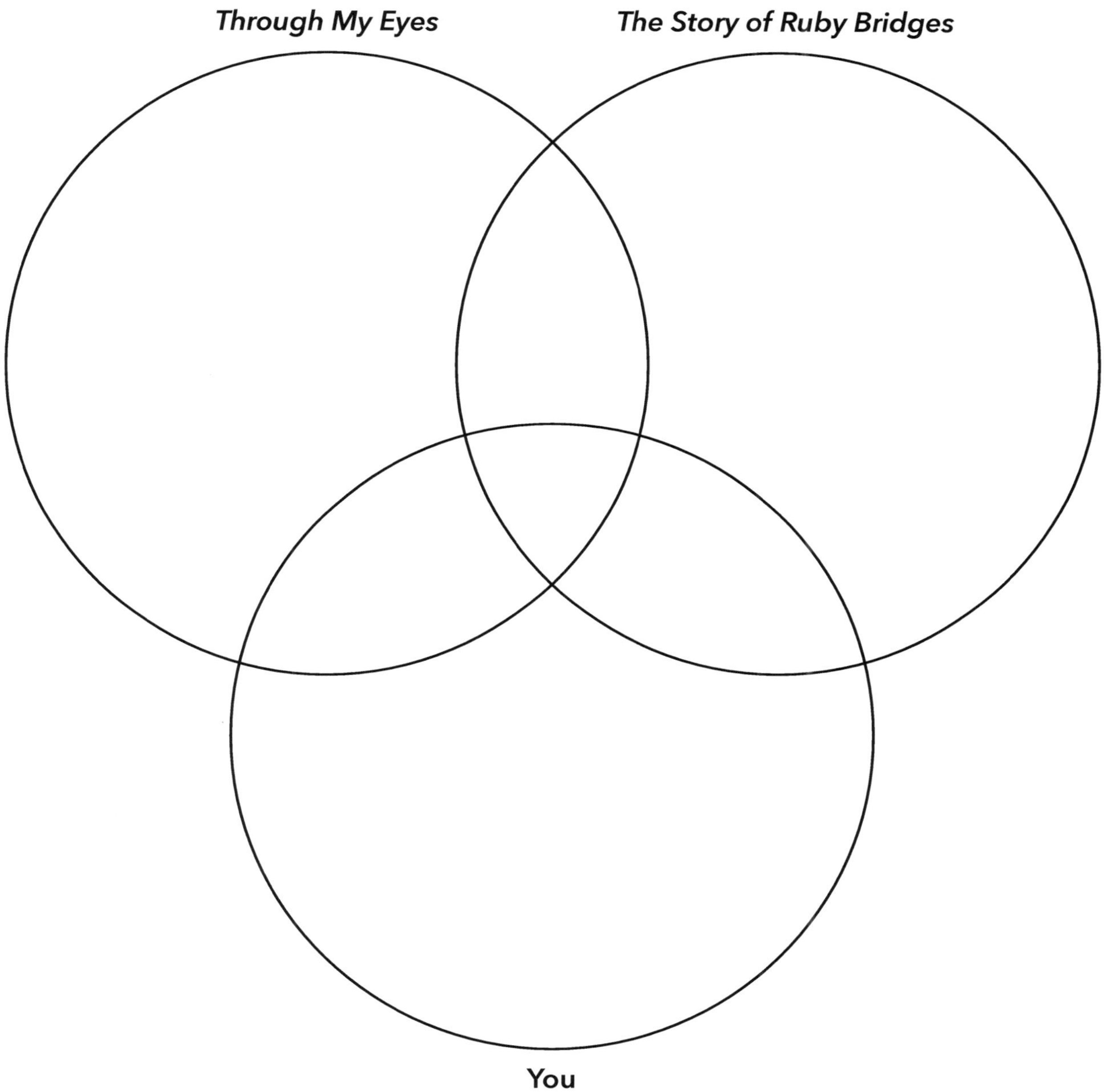

Perseverance

Extend Your Thinking

What are some character traits that are needed in order to persevere through life challenges? Use your thoughts from your Venn diagram to help provide evidence for your position in an extended response essay.

Include the following in your response:

1. a clear message outlining at least three character traits that can help people persevere through life's challenges,
2. evidence from both texts and your personal life, and
3. strong essay organization with a clear introduction, body, and conclusion.

NAME:______________________________ DATE:______________

LESSON 4.4 RUBRIC
Traits of Perseverance

	Exceeds Expectations 5 points	**Proficient 4 points**	**Developed 3 points**	**Emerging 2 points**	**Novice 1 point**
Content	Includes a clear message outlining at least four character traits that help people persevere through life's challenges.	Includes a clear message outlining three character traits that help people persevere through life's challenges.	Includes a clear message outlining two character traits that help people persevere through life's challenges.	Includes a clear message outlining a character trait that helps people persevere through life's challenges.	Includes a clear message outlining what character traits help people persevere through life's challenges.
Supporting Evidence	Character traits are clearly supported through multiple examples from both texts and the student's personal life.	Character traits are supported through multiple examples from both texts and the student's personal life.	Character traits are clearly supported through only one example from both texts and the student's personal life.	Character traits are clearly supported through an example from both texts.	Character traits are clearly supported through an example from the student's personal life.
Organization	Has strong organization with a compelling introduction, evidence-supported body, and a solid conclusion.	Has strong organization with an introduction, evidence-supported body, and conclusion.	Has strong organization with an introduction, body, and conclusion.	Introduction or conclusion is missing.	Does not have a clear introduction or conclusion.
Conventions	Demonstrates superior command of the conventions of the English language, with no errors in grammar, spelling, or usage.	Demonstrates command of the conventions of the English language, with no more than one error in grammar, spelling, or usage.	Demonstrates command of the conventions of the English language, with no more than two errors in grammar, spelling, or usage.	Demonstrates command of the conventions of the English language, with no more than three errors in grammar, spelling, or usage.	Demonstrates novice command of the conventions of the English language, with more than three errors in grammar, spelling, or usage.
					________ / 16

LESSON 4.5

Flying High With Perseverance

Common Core State Standards

- RL.3.1
- RL.3.2
- RL.3.4
- RL.3.5
- RL.3.6
- RL.3.10
- RF.3.4
- W.3.3
- W.3.4
- W.3.5
- W.3.6
- W.3.10
- SL.3.1
- SL.3.2
- SL.3.6
- L.3.1
- L.3.2
- L.3.3
- L.3.4
- L.3.5
- L.3.6

Materials

- Lesson 4.5 Literature Analysis Model
- Lesson 4.5 Poetry Analysis
- Lesson 4.5 Poem Brainstorming
- Lesson 4.5 Rubric: Poetry Reading
- Student copies of "Fireflies" by Paul Fleischman
- Student copies of "Democracy" by Langston Hughes

Estimated Time

- 160 minutes

Objectives

In this lesson, students will:

- analyze poetry to determine the meaning of nonliteral language as it is used in a text, and
- use multiple sources to support thoughts on a certain topic.

Content

Students will read two poems, "Fireflies" by Paul Fleischman and "Democracy" by Langston Hughes, to help them analyze the author's use of figurative language to create meaning. Students will use their knowledge of the mentor authors' craft and knowledge gained from poems and other readings in this unit to help them write a poem about what perseverance means to them.

Prior Knowledge

Students will need experience identifying and analyzing poetry. Students will also need to know how to identify figurative language and the meaning of words or phrases as they are used in the text.

INSTRUCTIONAL SEQUENCE

1. Explain to students that today they will read two poems. Beforehand, have students do a quick brainstorm with their table group members, taking turns writing down characteristics of poems for a minute. Clarify or review any information as needed.
2. Have students read "Fireflies" by Paul Fleischman with a partner. For an initial analysis, work with the students to complete Lesson 4.5 Literature Analysis Model. Consider leaving certain boxes blank, depending on the focus of this lesson.
3. After their initial reading, students should analyze the poem for descriptive and figurative language, as well as literary devices that add to the beauty of the poem, using Lesson 4.5 Poetry Analysis.
4. Afterward, have students read "Democracy" by Langston Hughes with their partner. For an initial analysis, work with the students to complete Lesson 4.5 Literature Analysis Model. Consider leaving certain boxes blank, depending on the focus of this lesson. Then, have students work on the questions for this poem on Lesson 4.5 Poetry Analysis. (See pp. 3–4 for additional information about using the Literature Analysis Model.)
5. Once students have completed reading both poems and all questions on Lesson 4.5 Poetry Analysis, hold a brief discussion about the questions so that students can hear other viewpoints. Students may add to their notes as needed.
6. Explain to students that they will use their knowledge and insights from this lesson, as well as the other lessons in this unit, to write a poem in the style of either Paul Fleischman or Langston Hughes regarding what perseverance means to them. Have students use Lesson 4.5 Poem Brainstorming to consider ideas, literary devices to be used, and the structure of the poem. They will perform this at a poetry reading for their parents or another class to share what they have learned in this unit. Students should use Lesson 4.5 Rubric: Poetry Reading to make sure they understand everything that is expected of them and their poem.

Teacher's Note. Consider modeling the techniques of each poet to write a poem if students have not had much practice writing in either style.

7. Students will need to work with a peer in order to practice speaking poetry fluently and with expression for the poetry reading. During this time, work with pairs to help students edit their poems or with public speaking.

Extension Activities

Students may:

- create an interpretive dance to accompany their poem,
- compose a musical score to accompany their poem, or
- create a unique piece of art to accompany their poem.

NAME:____ DATE:____________________

LESSON 4.5

Literature Analysis Model

Directions: Complete this Literature Analysis Model about the poem assigned.

	Chosen or Assigned Text: ________________________
Key Words	
Important Ideas	
Tone	
Mood	
Imagery	
Symbolism	
Structure of Writing	

Note. Adapted from *Exploring America in the 1950s* (p. 10) by M. Sandling & K. L. Chandler, 2014, Waco, TX: Prufrock Press. Copyright 2014 by Center for Gifted Education. Adapted with permission.

Perseverance

NAME: ______________________ DATE: ____________

Perseverance

LESSON 4.5

Poetry Analysis

Directions: Use the following chart to help guide your analysis of "Fireflies" by Paul Fleischman. Then use the questions to analyze "Democracy" by Langston Hughes. Be sure to support your thoughts with evidence from each poem.

"Fireflies" by Paul Fleischman

Literary Device	How Does the Literary Device Help Describe the Characteristics of Fireflies?
Alliteration	
Repetition	
Personification	
Metaphor	

"Democracy" by Langston Hughes

1. Consider the ideas in each of the stanzas. How does each stanza build upon the previous one?

2. How does the speaker's sense of urgency grow as the poem continues?

3. How does the third stanza symbolize the long struggle of the speaker and the people who came before him or her?

4. What does this poem say about the positives and negatives of perseverance?

NAME:______________________________ DATE:______________

Perseverance

LESSON 4.5

Poem Brainstorming

Possible topics (times I persevered):
Possible titles:
Important ideas about how I persevered:

Literary Devices to Use	How to Use the Device In My Poem
Alliteration	
Repetition	
Personification	
Metaphor	
Ideas for Structure of the Poem	

NAME:________________________________ DATE:______________

LESSON 4.5 RUBRIC

Poetry Reading

	Exceeds Expectations 5 points	Proficient 4 points	Developed 3 points	Emerging 2 points	Novice 1 point
Ideas in Poem	Created in the style of one of the mentor authors and uses personal details to describe what perseverance means to the student.	Created in the style of one of the mentor authors to describe what perseverance means to the student.	Created in the style of one of the mentor authors and vaguely describes what perseverance means to the student.	Describes what perseverance means to the student.	Created in the style of one of the mentor authors, but does not reflect the student's views on perseverance.
Figurative Language	Contains at least four different types of figurative language to effectively create meaning in the poem.	Contains three different types of figurative language to effectively create meaning in the poem.	Contains two different types of figurative language to effectively create meaning in the poem.	Contains only one type of figurative language to effectively create meaning in the poem.	Lacks the use of figurative language used to create meaning.
Conventions	Demonstrates superior command of the conventions of the English language, with no errors in grammar, spelling, or usage.	Demonstrates command of the conventions of the English language, with no more than one error in grammar, spelling, or usage.	Demonstrates command of the conventions of the English language, with no more than two errors in grammar, spelling, or usage.	Demonstrates command of the conventions of the English language, with no more than three errors in grammar, spelling, or usage.	Demonstrates novice command of the conventions of the English language, with more than three errors in grammar, spelling, or usage.
Speaking	Student performed the poem in a fluid manner in an understandable voice, using inflection and pauses for dramatic effect.	Student performed the poem in a fluid manner in an understandable voice, using inflection or pauses for dramatic effect.	Student performed the poem in a fluid manner in an understandable voice.	Student performed the poem in a fluid manner.	Student performed the poem in a way that was not fluid or understandable.
					________ / 16

NAME:______________________________ DATE:______________

UNIT IV

Culminating Essay Prompt

Directions: In this unit, you read about different people and different characters persevering under various circumstances. Describe what you have learned about persevering. Include information about how you might approach problems in the future, given what you have learned.

ANSWER KEY

Lesson 1.1 Thinking While Analyzing Poetry

Answers are in bold.

Example of Figurative Language	Stanza and Line Where Example Is Found	How the Author's Use of This Language Adds Meaning to the Poem
Alliteration: "swig of soda," "slow slither of snow cone syrup," "balloon of bubble gum"	**7, 8–9, 5**	**Provides for easy flow and rhythm in poem.**
Onomatopoeia: "crack"	**6**	**Add voice to the poem.**
Personification: "it yells," "running down your arm"	**16, 11**	**Adds imagery to the poem.**

Lesson 1.2 Comparing and Contrasting With Allen Say

Chart answers will vary.

1. Both settings are in America and show images of the American West, specifically desert landscapes.
2. Character traits for grandfather: loyal, traditional, eager; character traits for both: brave, courageous, adventurous; character traits for the boy: artistic, talented, hopeful.
3. Both central messages focus on following your dreams and making choices that can change one's life. The central messages differ in that in *Grandfather's Journey*, the message encourages the reader to return to one's roots while *The Sign Painter* encourages readers to learn what they can and continue to move toward learning more and experiencing more of life.
4. Answers will vary, but students should refer to the character traits listed in the Venn diagram for Question 2.

Lesson 1.3 Learning About Lincoln

1. Answers will vary, but may include that first Lincoln was born in a small town without much money. Then he traveled and earned a living as a lawyer, making him very wealthy. After that, Lincoln became a senator to represent his state in Washington, DC. Next, Lincoln was elected president of the United States during the Civil War. Finally, Lincoln was assassinated while watching a play in Ford's Theatre.
2. Answers will vary, but may include that the author mentions that Lincoln was careless about his appearance, but as president, he always looked professional, or that Lincoln was not very educated, but grew into one of the most eloquent speakers of the time.

3. Answers will vary, but may include that Lincoln had very simple beginnings, but came to be one of the most important people in the country as president; however, he still kept many of his similar traits, such as inviting friends to the White House to "stay a spell."
4. Answers will vary, but may include that the pictures give the reader a look into the past of how people dressed, in which type of home Lincoln lived, and how Lincoln changed over the years.
5. Answers will vary, but students should note that the captions give the reader more insight into the life of Abraham Lincoln.
6. Answers will vary, but students may suggest adding text boxes or a glossary to help with definitions of unfamiliar terms or words.

Lesson 1.4 Fables and Morals

1. Answers will vary based on the fable chosen by the student pairs.
2. a–e. Answers will vary based on the fable chosen by the student pairs.

Lesson 2.1 Exploring Giovanni Poetry

1. Most lines begin with "and." This allows for a smooth and continuous read that helps the reader flow easily through the poem.
2. The length of each line is relatively short, with the longest lines representing a new tradition being described. This possibly helps the reader see the ideas as one continuous tradition that is filled with special events.
3. The poem is written in free verse with no apparent rhyme scheme or stanzas. The author may have chosen this to help the reader see all of the small activities as a smaller piece of a large whole that is the summer in this area.
4. Answers will vary, but students may mention that because the poem is written in one continuous stanza, the author allows the reader to flow effortlessly through the traditions of this summer in Knoxville, TN.

Lesson 2.2 World Village Exploration

1. The book's main idea is to inform the reader about our world's cultures.
2. Answers are in bold.

Word	Page Number	My Definition	Reason for My Definition	Actual Meaning of the Word
Population	**7**	**Answers will vary.**	**Answers will vary.**	**The total number of persons inhabiting a city.**
Village	**8**	**Answers will vary.**	**Answers will vary.**	**A small community in a rural area.**
Global	**12**	**Answers will vary.**	**Answers will vary.**	**Pertaining to the whole world.**
Babel	**10**	**Answers will vary.**	**Answers will vary.**	**A confused mixture of sounds or voices.**

3. Answers will vary, but students should note that there are fewer very young and very old, with more people in the ages that fall in between.
4. Answers will vary, but students may mention that resources would be stretched and people may have access to fewer and fewer resources as more people live longer.
5. Answers will vary, but students may note that the illustrations are very colorful to represent the many different cultures of our world or that the illustrations are busy to represent the constant action occurring in our world.

Lesson 2.3 Cultural Traditions

Answers are in bold.

Guiding Questions	*Throw Your Tooth on the Roof* by Selby Beeler	*Art Around the World* by Heather Leonard	*What the World Eats* by Faith D'Aluisio
How are the cultural traditions or customs presented in this book similar to your cultural traditions or customs?	**Answers will vary, but students should notice that all cultures have some custom of what to do with a lost tooth.**	**Answers will vary, but students should notice that art reflects the values of the cultures.**	**Answers will vary, but students may notice that most countries may eat fruit.**
How are the cultural traditions or customs presented in this book different from your cultural traditions or customs?	**Answers will vary, but students may notice that some cultures throw teeth on/over the roof, leave teeth in shoes, or plant teeth in the ground (many more).**	**Answers will vary, but students should notice that the materials available for art varies according to what is available locally.**	**Answers will vary, but students should notice that some countries use only locally grown items while others import items.**
How do the illustrations in this book help support the differences and similarities between cultural traditions or customs?	**Answers will vary, but students should notice that the illustrations support the main similarities and differences written in the text.**	**Answers will vary, but students should notice that the illustrations support the main similarities and differences written in the text.**	**Answers will vary, but students should notice that the illustrations support the main similarities and differences written in the text.**

Extend Your Thinking: Questions to Consider

1–3. Answers will vary.

Lesson 2.4 Medieval Feast

1. Answers are in bold.

Word/ Phrase	Page Number	My Definition	Reason for My Definition	Actual Meaning of the Word
Marzipan	**25**	**Answers will vary.**	**Answers will vary.**	**A confection made of almonds reduced to a paste with sugar and often molded into various shapes.**
Turned on Spits	**16**	**Answers will vary.**	**Answers will vary.**	**The boar was placed on a stick that rotated the meat evenly above the fire.**
Member of His Court	**4**	**Answers will vary.**	**Answers will vary.**	**People who traveled with and waited on the king.**
Embroidered	**7**	**Answers will vary.**	**Answers will vary.**	**Decorated with ornamental needlework.**
Estate	**5**	**Answers will vary.**	**Answers will vary.**	**A large piece of property.**

2. Answers are in bold.

Social Class/Job	Page Number	My Thoughts	Reason for My Thoughts	Actual Explanation of Social Class/Job
Serf	**5**	**Answers will vary.**	**Answers will vary.**	**People who lived on a lord's land who served the lord in return for a place to live.**
Ewerer	**21**	**Answers will vary.**	**Answers will vary.**	**A worker who brought and heated water for nobles.**
Scullion Boy	**15**	**Answers will vary.**	**Answers will vary.**	**A kitchen servant.**

3. Answers will vary.
4. Answers will vary, but should include sequencing words such as first, next, then, after, finally, last, and so forth.
5. Answers will vary, but students should notice that based on the preparations for meals such as a king's feast, mealtimes were of great importance. Students may wonder about "normal"

meals where the king was not present, so you could allow students to research to extend their knowledge.

6. a. Answers will vary, but students may notice that because homes were usually built with highly flammable materials, a kitchen was commonly separated for the safety of the residents; b. Answers will vary, but students may notice from the illustrations that the room is very large, with many ornamental decorations, along with a raised platform for important people.
7. Answers will vary.

Lesson 2.5 Cultures and Change

1. Answers will vary, but could include that of imagination, how cultures can change a person, cleverness, or creativity.
2. Answers will vary, but text evidence should support the central message chosen by the student in Question 1.
3. Answers will vary, but students should emphasize that Nicky is used to a life that is completely different from Grandma's.
4. Answers will vary, but students should emphasize Grandma's culture values nature, outdoors, and creativity.
5. Answers will vary, but students should note that Grandma is persistent in her suggestions to Nicky to make the most of his time spent there.

Lesson 3.1 Exploring Myths

1. Answers are in bold.

Myth Name	Element of Nature	How Element of Nature Is Explained	Supernatural or Magical Characteristics
Myths from Around the World: China	**The rule of the Huang Di Dynasty.**	**Answers will vary.**	**Answers will vary, but may include fog to cover a battlefield, giants, army of demons, person who could dry up rain.**
Pan Gu and Nü Wa	**The creation of Earth, the creation of humans.**	**Answers will vary.**	**Giant holds up heavens and Earth and eventually becomes part of the heavens and Earth. Goddess creates humans so she would not be lonely.**
Chinook Creation Myth	**Creation of the Chinook people.**	**Answers will vary.**	**People coming from eggs made by Thunderbird.**

Lesson 3.1 The Process of a Seed Becoming a Plant

1. Answers will vary, but students should notice that because the seed is planted below the ground and out of human sight, what happens during the growth process is not always visible and must require some belief in the scientific explanations around how the seed transforms into a plant.
2. Answers will vary, but students should have seed to seedling to roots and shoots to plant.

3. Answers will vary, but students should include the following vocabulary terms of the life cycle of a plant using similar sequencing words: Seed: first; Sprout: next, then, after, etc.; Roots: next, then, after, etc.; Shoots: next, then, after, etc.; Plant: finally, last.
4. Answers will vary, but students may mention that people would make up stories of why a seed that was planted in the ground grew to be a full plant. Students may mention that people might have said it was due to gods or that good fortune helped to grow seeds to plants.
5. Answers will vary, but may include: cause: place seed in a warm, wet area; effect: roots and shoots begin to grow; or cause: plant seed in moist soil; effect: plant begins to grow.
6. Answers will vary.

Lesson 3.2 Space Exploration

1. Answers will vary, but students should note that the main idea is about the importance of space exploration or the belief of all of the workers during the Apollo 11 mission that they were doing something to help all of mankind.
2. Answers will vary, but students should note that the article is mostly informing about the mission of MAVEN.
3. Answers will vary, but students should note that space travel is treated similarly by explaining the time it takes to prepare for a space mission. It is treated differently because the book focuses more on the people of the mission, while the web article focuses only on the scientific factors of the mission.
4. Answers will vary, but students should notice that because we were successful in our mission to the moon, going farther to explore Mars is possible.

Lesson 3.3 The Power of Poetry

"Your World"

1. Answers will vary.
2. Answers will vary, but students should notice that in the first stanza, the speaker felt small and insignificant, but began to feel more confident in the second stanza.
3. Answers will vary.
4. Answers will vary, but should focus around the message of believing in oneself.

"Try, Try Again"

1. Answers will vary, but students should note that the speaker of the poem wants people to believe in themselves enough to continue to try even after failure.
2. Answers will vary, but students should note that the speaker would encourage people to continue to try even when things seem to get in the way.
3. Answers will vary.

Lesson 3.4 Examining for Beliefs

1–4. Answers will vary based on newspaper article chosen.

Lesson 4.1 Character Perseverance

Answers for webs will vary.

1. Answers will vary, but students may note that the protagonist is loyal, brave, dedicated, and a good problem solver.

2. Answers will vary, but students should note that Gaylen's problem solving is the key to his success.
3. Answers will vary, but students may note how his loyalty and dedication to the task helped him to problem-solve during any obstacles he encountered.
4. Answers will vary.
5. Answers will vary.

Lesson 4.2 Developing the Central Message

Thoughts: Answers will vary, but students may notice that Elmer continually tried to think of ways to outsmart the animals that tried to stop him on his way to free the dragon.

Words: Answers will vary, but students may mention the scene in which Elmer talks to the lion to distract him from his anger and desire to eat Elmer.

Actions: Answers will vary, but students may mention the scene in which Elmer gives the rhino his toothbrush to distract him from his desire to harm Elmer.

Feelings: Answers will vary, but students could mention how father was afraid that the mouse would tell someone he was on the island.

Lesson 4.3 Persevere for a Cause

1. Answers will vary, but students may mention that because he was willing to skate for 11 days to reach Washington, DC, to protest for equal rights.
2. Answers will vary, but students should notice that Dr. King would not stop fighting for the cause he believed in even in the face of threats or jail.
3. Answers will vary, but students should note that many thousands of people were willing to gather in the August heat to protest for civil rights. Many even traveled from all across the country, held marches elsewhere, and faced threats or imprisonment in order to campaign for equal rights.
4. Answers will vary, but students should note that approximately one year later, the Civil Rights Act was passed, which outlawed discrimination based on race.

Extend Your Thinking

Answers will vary, but students should understand that many African Americans felt the need to campaign for equal civil rights no matter the costs. Students may cite examples of the man who skated to DC, the people who walked from New York to DC, the thousands of people who gathered in the heat of Washington Mall to hear Dr. King's speech, the fact that many had protested for years for these rights, or examples of wanting equal access to public facilities.

Lesson 4.4 Character Trait Venn Diagram

Answers will vary for the Venn diagram, but students may mention that Ruby continued to go to school each day even though people were yelling at her and threatening her life (bravery), she continued to attend school even though she was the only one in her class (dedication), she smiled each day while learning (positivity), or that she prayed for those who yelled at her (kindness).

Extend Your Thinking

Answers will vary.

Lesson 4.5 Poetry Analysis

"Fireflies" by Paul Fleischman

Answers are in bold.

Literary Device	How Does the Literary Device Help Describe the Characteristics of Fireflies?
Alliteration	**Fireflies flickering flitting flashing fireflies; Glimmering gleaming, glowing.**
Repetition	**Key words such as "night," "fireflies," and "light."**
Personification	**Insect calligraphers practicing penmanship, fine artists in flight adding dabs of light**
Metaphor	**Insect calligraphers; fine artists.**

"Democracy" by Langston Hughes

1. Each stanza shows the author's belief that something needs to change. The author begins by setting up the situation that needs to change, continues to explain why things must change, and then offers a hope for the changed future.
2. The speaker's tone becomes more and more serious as the poem continues through figurative language.
3. This stanza indicates that people continuously state that things will work out in the end, but the speaker wants the reader to know that persistence is key to make tomorrow's promises today's reality.
4. The poem shows that although people have been waiting patiently for things to "take their course," it is important to the "survival" of everyone to take action today.

REFERENCES

Baskin, B. H., & Harris, K. H. (1980). *Books for the gifted child.* New York, NY: Bowker.

Center for Gifted Education. (2004). *Exploring nonfiction: Questions and organizers to guide reading and understanding nonfiction texts.* Williamsburg, VA: Author.

Center for Gifted Education. (2011). *Guide to teaching language arts for high-ability students.* Dubuque, IA: Kendall Hunt.

Harvey, S., & Goudvis, A. (2007). *Strategies that work: Teaching comprehension for understanding and engagement.* Portland, ME: Stenhouse.

McKeague, P. M. (2009). *Writing about literature: Step by step.* Dubuque, IA: Kendall Hunt.

National Governors Association Center for Best Practices, & Council of Chief State School Officers. (2010). *Common Core State Standards for English language arts.* Washington, DC: Authors.

Sandling, M., & Chandler, K. L. (2014). *Exploring America in the 1950s.* Waco, TX: Prufrock Press.

ABOUT THE AUTHOR

Molly Bryan Talbot is a special education teacher of third- and fourth-grade gifted students at Zachary Elementary School in the Zachary Community School District in Louisiana. Molly attended Louisiana State University, where she earned her bachelor's and master's degrees in elementary education, grades pre-K–5, through the LSU Holmes Program. She then returned to LSU to earn her education specialist degree in gifted education. Molly currently resides in Baton Rouge, LA, with her husband, David. She is the author of *Challenging Common Core Math Lessons: Activities and Extensions for Gifted and Advanced Learners in Grade 4*.

COMMON CORE STATE STANDARDS ALIGNMENT

Lesson	Common Core State Standards
Lesson 1.1	RL.3.1 Ask and answer questions to demonstrate understanding of a text, referring explicitly to the text as the basis for the answers.
	RL.3.4 Determine the meaning of words and phrases as they are used in a text, distinguishing literal from nonliteral language.
	RL.3.5 Refer to parts of stories, dramas, and poems when writing or speaking about a text, using terms such as chapter, scene, and stanza; describe how each successive part builds on earlier sections.
	RF.3.4a Read grade-level text with purpose and understanding. W.3.4 With guidance and support from adults, produce writing in which the development and organization are appropriate to task and purpose.
	W.3.5 With guidance and support from peers and adults, develop and strengthen writing as needed by planning, revising, and editing.
	W.3.6 With guidance and support from adults, use technology to produce and publish writing (using keyboarding skills) as well as to interact and collaborate with others.
	W.3.8 Recall information from experiences or gather information from print and digital sources; take brief notes on sources and sort evidence into provided categories.
	SL.3.1 Engage effectively in a range of collaborative discussions (one-on-one, in groups, and teacher-led) with diverse partners on grade 3 topics and texts, building on others' ideas and expressing their own clearly.
	SL.3.4 Report on a topic or text, tell a story, or recount an experience with appropriate facts and relevant, descriptive details, speaking clearly at an understandable pace.
	SL.3.5 Create engaging audio recordings of stories or poems that demonstrate fluid reading at an understandable pace; add visual displays when appropriate to emphasize or enhance certain facts or details.

Lesson	Common Core State Standards
Lesson 1.1, *continued*	SL.3.6 Speak in complete sentences when appropriate to task and situation in order to provide requested detail or clarification. (See grade 3 Language standards 1 and 3 here for specific expectations.)
	L.3.1 Demonstrate command of the conventions of standard English grammar and usage when writing or speaking.
	L.3.3 Use knowledge of language and its conventions when writing, speaking, reading, or listening.
	L.3.5 Demonstrate understanding of figurative language, word relationships and nuances in word meanings.
Lesson 1.2	RL.3.1 Ask and answer questions to demonstrate understanding of a text, referring explicitly to the text as the basis for the answers.
	RL.3.9 Compare and contrast the themes, settings, and plots of stories written by the same author about the same or similar characters (e.g., in books from a series).
	RL.3.10 By the end of the year, read and comprehend literature, including stories, dramas, and poetry, at the high end of the grades 2–3 text complexity band independently and proficiently.
	W.3.4 With guidance and support from adults, produce writing in which the development and organization are appropriate to task and purpose.
	W.3.10 Write routinely over extended time frames (time for research, reflection, and revision) and shorter time frames (a single sitting or a day or two) for a range of discipline-specific tasks, purposes, and audiences.
	SL.3.1 Engage effectively in a range of collaborative discussions (one-on-one, in groups, and teacher-led) with diverse partners on grade 3 topics and texts, building on others' ideas and expressing their own clearly.
	SL.3.4 Report on a topic or text, tell a story, or recount an experience with appropriate facts and relevant, descriptive details, speaking clearly at an understandable pace.
	SL.3.6 Speak in complete sentences when appropriate to task and situation in order to provide requested detail or clarification. (See grade 3 Language standards 1 and 3 here for specific expectations.)
	L.3.1 Demonstrate command of the conventions of standard English grammar and usage when writing or speaking.
	L.3.2 Demonstrate command of the conventions of standard English capitalization, punctuation, and spelling when writing.

Lesson	Common Core State Standards
Lesson 1.2, *continued*	L.3.3 Use knowledge of language and its conventions when writing, speaking, reading, or listening.
Lesson 1.3	RI.3.3 Describe the relationship between a series of historical events, scientific ideas or concepts, or steps in technical procedures in a text, using language that pertains to time, sequence, and cause/effect.
	RI.3.5 Use text features and search tools (e.g., key words, sidebars, hyperlinks) to locate information relevant to a given topic efficiently.
	RI.3.7 Use information gained from illustrations (e.g., maps, photographs) and the words in a text to demonstrate understanding of the text (e.g., where, when, why, and how key events occur).
	RI.3.8 Describe the logical connection between particular sentences and paragraphs in a text (e.g., comparison, cause/effect, first/second/third in a sequence).
	RI.3.9 Compare and contrast the most important points and key details presented in two texts on the same topic.
	RI.3.10 By the end of the year, read and comprehend informational texts, including history/social studies, science, and technical texts, at the high end of the grades 2–3 text complexity band independently and proficiently.
	W.3.7 Conduct short research projects that build knowledge about a topic.
	W.3.8 Recall information from experiences or gather information from print and digital sources; take brief notes on sources and sort evidence into provided categories.
	SL.3.1 Engage effectively in a range of collaborative discussions (one-on-one, in groups, and teacher-led) with diverse partners on grade 3 topics and texts, building on others' ideas and expressing their own clearly.
	SL.3.4 Report on a topic or text, tell a story, or recount an experience with appropriate facts and relevant, descriptive details, speaking clearly at an understandable pace.
	SL.3.6 Speak in complete sentences when appropriate to task and situation in order to provide requested detail or clarification. (See grade 3 Language standards 1 and 3 here for specific expectations.)
	L.3.1 Demonstrate command of the conventions of standard English grammar and usage when writing or speaking.

Lesson	Common Core State Standards
Lesson 1.3, *continued*	L.3.2 Demonstrate command of the conventions of standard English capitalization, punctuation, and spelling when writing.
	L.3.3 Use knowledge of language and its conventions when writing, speaking, reading, or listening.
Lesson 1.4	RL.3.2 Recount stories, including fables, folktales, and myths from diverse cultures; determine the central message, lesson, or moral and explain how it is conveyed through key details in the text.
	RL.3.3 Describe characters in a story (e.g., their traits, motivations, or feelings) and explain how their actions contribute to the sequence of events.
	RL.3.6 Distinguish their own point of view from that of the narrator or those of the characters.
	W.3.1 Write opinion pieces on topics or texts, supporting a point of view with reasons.
	W.3.8 Recall information from experiences or gather information from print and digital sources; take brief notes on sources and sort evidence into provided categories.
	W.3.10 Write routinely over extended time frames (time for research, reflection, and revision) and shorter time frames (a single sitting or a day or two) for a range of discipline-specific tasks, purposes, and audiences.
	SL.3.1 Engage effectively in a range of collaborative discussions (one-on-one, in groups, and teacher-led) with diverse partners on grade 3 topics and texts, building on others' ideas and expressing their own clearly.
	SL.3.4 Report on a topic or text, tell a story, or recount an experience with appropriate facts and relevant, descriptive details, speaking clearly at an understandable pace.
	SL.3.6 Speak in complete sentences when appropriate to task and situation in order to provide requested detail or clarification. (See grade 3 Language standards 1 and 3 here for specific expectations.)
	L.3.1 Demonstrate command of the conventions of standard English grammar and usage when writing or speaking.
	L.3.2 Demonstrate command of the conventions of standard English capitalization, punctuation, and spelling when writing.
	L.3.3 Use knowledge of language and its conventions when writing, speaking, reading, or listening.

Lesson	Common Core State Standards
Lesson 2.1	RL.3.10 By the end of the year, read and comprehend literature, including stories, dramas, and poetry, at the high end of the grades 2–3 text complexity band independently and proficiently.
	RF.3.3 Know and apply grade-level phonics and word analysis skills in decoding words.
	RF.3.4 Read with sufficient accuracy and fluency to support comprehension.
	W.3.4 With guidance and support from adults, produce writing in which the development and organization are appropriate to task and purpose.
	W.3.10 Write routinely over extended time frames (time for research, reflection, and revision) and shorter time frames (a single sitting or a day or two) for a range of discipline-specific tasks, purposes, and audiences.
	SL.3.1 Engage effectively in a range of collaborative discussions (one-on-one, in groups, and teacher-led) with diverse partners on grade 3 topics and texts, building on others' ideas and expressing their own clearly.
	SL.3.2 Determine the main ideas and supporting details of a text read aloud or information presented in diverse media and formats, including visually, quantitatively, and orally.
	SL.3.3 Ask and answer questions about information from a speaker, offering appropriate elaboration and detail.
	SL.3.6 Speak in complete sentences when appropriate to task and situation in order to provide requested detail or clarification. (See grade 3 Language standards 1 and 3 here for specific expectations.)
	L.3.1 Demonstrate command of the conventions of standard English grammar and usage when writing or speaking.
	L.3.2 Demonstrate command of the conventions of standard English capitalization, punctuation, and spelling when writing.
	L.3.3 Use knowledge of language and its conventions when writing, speaking, reading, or listening.
	L.3.6 Acquire and use accurately grade-appropriate conversational, general academic, and domain-specific words and phrases, including those that signal spatial and temporal relationships (e.g., After dinner that night we went looking for them).
Lesson 2.2	RI.3.1 Ask and answer questions to demonstrate understanding of a text, referring explicitly to the text as the basis for the answers.

Lesson	Common Core State Standards
Lesson 2.2, *continued*	RI.3.2 Determine the main idea of a text; recount the key details and explain how they support the main idea.
	RI.3.3 Describe the relationship between a series of historical events, scientific ideas or concepts, or steps in technical procedures in a text, using language that pertains to time, sequence, and cause/effect.
	RI.3.7 Use information gained from illustrations (e.g., maps, photographs) and the words in a text to demonstrate understanding of the text (e.g., where, when, why, and how key events occur).
	RI.3.8 Describe the logical connection between particular sentences and paragraphs in a text (e.g., comparison, cause/effect, first/second/third in a sequence).
	W.3.7 Conduct short research projects that build knowledge about a topic.
	W.3.8 Recall information from experiences or gather information from print and digital sources; take brief notes on sources and sort evidence into provided categories.
	W.3.10 Write routinely over extended time frames (time for research, reflection, and revision) and shorter time frames (a single sitting or a day or two) for a range of discipline-specific tasks, purposes, and audiences.
	L.3.1 Demonstrate command of the conventions of standard English grammar and usage when writing or speaking.
	L.3.2 Demonstrate command of the conventions of standard English capitalization, punctuation, and spelling when writing.
	L.3.3 Use knowledge of language and its conventions when writing, speaking, reading, or listening.
Lesson 2.3	RI.3.1 Ask and answer questions to demonstrate understanding of a text, referring explicitly to the text as the basis for the answers.
	RI.3.2 Determine the main idea of a text; recount the key details and explain how they support the main idea.
	RI.3.5 Use text features and search tools (e.g., key words, sidebars, hyperlinks) to locate information relevant to a given topic efficiently.
	RI.3.7 Use information gained from illustrations (e.g., maps, photographs) and the words in a text to demonstrate understanding of the text (e.g., where, when, why, and how key events occur).

Lesson	Common Core State Standards
Lesson 2.3, *continued*	RI.3.9 Compare and contrast the most important points and key details presented in two texts on the same topic.
	RI.3.10 By the end of the year, read and comprehend informational texts, including history/social studies, science, and technical texts, at the high end of the grades 2–3 text complexity band independently and proficiently.
	W.3.2 Write informative/explanatory texts to examine a topic and convey ideas and information clearly.
	W.3.7 Conduct short research projects that build knowledge about a topic.
	W.3.8 Recall information from experiences or gather information from print and digital sources; take brief notes on sources and sort evidence into provided categories.
	W.3.10 Write routinely over extended time frames (time for research, reflection, and revision) and shorter time frames (a single sitting or a day or two) for a range of discipline-specific tasks, purposes, and audiences.
	L.3.1 Demonstrate command of the conventions of standard English grammar and usage when writing or speaking.
	L.3.2 Demonstrate command of the conventions of standard English capitalization, punctuation, and spelling when writing.
	L.3.3 Use knowledge of language and its conventions when writing, speaking, reading, or listening.
Lesson 2.4	RI.3.4 Determine the meaning of general academic and domain-specific words and phrases in a text relevant to a grade 3 topic or subject area.
	RI.3.7 Use information gained from illustrations (e.g., maps, photographs) and the words in a text to demonstrate understanding of the text (e.g., where, when, why, and how key events occur).
	RI.3.8 Describe the logical connection between particular sentences and paragraphs in a text (e.g., comparison, cause/effect, first/second/third in a sequence).
	W.3.2 Write informative/explanatory texts to examine a topic and convey ideas and information clearly.
	W.3.4 With guidance and support from adults, produce writing in which the development and organization are appropriate to task and purpose.
	W.3.7 Conduct short research projects that build knowledge about a topic.

Lesson	Common Core State Standards
Lesson 2.4, *continued*	W.3.8 Recall information from experiences or gather information from print and digital sources; take brief notes on sources and sort evidence into provided categories.
	W.3.10 Write routinely over extended time frames (time for research, reflection, and revision) and shorter time frames (a single sitting or a day or two) for a range of discipline-specific tasks, purposes, and audiences.
	SL.3.1 Engage effectively in a range of collaborative discussions (one-on-one, in groups, and teacher-led) with diverse partners on grade 3 topics and texts, building on others' ideas and expressing their own clearly.
	SL.3.2 Determine the main ideas and supporting details of a text read aloud or information presented in diverse media and formats, including visually, quantitatively, and orally.
	SL.3.6 Speak in complete sentences when appropriate to task and situation in order to provide requested detail or clarification. (See grade 3 Language standards 1 and 3 here for specific expectations.)
	L.3.1 Demonstrate command of the conventions of standard English grammar and usage when writing or speaking.
	L.3.2 Demonstrate command of the conventions of standard English capitalization, punctuation, and spelling when writing.
	L.3.3 Use knowledge of language and its conventions when writing, speaking, reading, or listening.
	L.3.4 Determine or clarify the meaning of unknown and multiple-meaning word and phrases based on grade 3 reading and content, choosing flexibly from a range of strategies.
Lesson 2.5	RL.3.1 Ask and answer questions to demonstrate understanding of a text, referring explicitly to the text as the basis for the answers.
	RL.3.2 Recount stories, including fables, folktales, and myths from diverse cultures; determine the central message, lesson, or moral and explain how it is conveyed through key details in the text.
	RL.3.3 Describe characters in a story (e.g., their traits, motivations, or feelings) and explain how their actions contribute to the sequence of events.
	RL.3.5 Refer to parts of stories, dramas, and poems when writing or speaking about a text, using terms such as chapter, scene, and stanza; describe how each successive part builds on earlier sections.

Lesson	Common Core State Standards
Lesson 2.5, *continued*	RL.3.7 Explain how specific aspects of a text's illustrations contribute to what is conveyed by the words in a story (e.g., create mood, emphasize aspects of a character or setting).
	RL.3.10 By the end of the year, read and comprehend literature, including stories, dramas, and poetry, at the high end of the grades 2–3 text complexity band independently and proficiently.
	W.3.3 Write narratives to develop real or imagined experiences or events using effective technique, descriptive details, and clear event sequences.
	W.3.10 Write routinely over extended time frames (time for research, reflection, and revision) and shorter time frames (a single sitting or a day or two) for a range of discipline-specific tasks, purposes, and audiences.
	SL.3.1 Engage effectively in a range of collaborative discussions (one-on-one, in groups, and teacher-led) with diverse partners on grade 3 topics and texts, building on others' ideas and expressing their own clearly.
	SL.3.2 Determine the main ideas and supporting details of a text read aloud or information presented in diverse media and formats, including visually, quantitatively, and orally.
	SL.3.6 Speak in complete sentences when appropriate to task and situation in order to provide requested detail or clarification. (See grade 3 Language standards 1 and 3 here for specific expectations.)
	L.3.1 Demonstrate command of the conventions of standard English grammar and usage when writing or speaking.
	L.3.2 Demonstrate command of the conventions of standard English capitalization, punctuation, and spelling when writing.
	L.3.3 Use knowledge of language and its conventions when writing, speaking, reading, or listening.
	L.3.4 Determine or clarify the meaning of unknown and multiple-meaning word and phrases based on grade 3 reading and content, choosing flexibly from a range of strategies.
Lesson 3.1	RI.3.1 Ask and answer questions to demonstrate understanding of a text, referring explicitly to the text as the basis for the answers.
	RI.3.3 Describe the relationship between a series of historical events, scientific ideas or concepts, or steps in technical procedures in a text, using language that pertains to time, sequence, and cause/effect.

Lesson	Common Core State Standards
Lesson 3.1, *continued*	RI.3.8 Describe the logical connection between particular sentences and paragraphs in a text (e.g., comparison, cause/effect, first/second/third in a sequence).
	RL.3.1 Ask and answer questions to demonstrate understanding of a text, referring explicitly to the text as the basis for the answers.
	RL.3.3 Describe characters in a story (e.g., their traits, motivations, or feelings) and explain how their actions contribute to the sequence of events.
	W.3.3 Write narratives to develop real or imagined experiences or events using effective technique, descriptive details, and clear event sequences.
	W.3.4 With guidance and support from adults, produce writing in which the development and organization are appropriate to task and purpose.
	W.3.5 With guidance and support from peers and adults, develop and strengthen writing as needed by planning, revising, and editing.
	W.3.10 Write routinely over extended time frames (time for research, reflection, and revision) and shorter time frames (a single sitting or a day or two) for a range of discipline-specific tasks, purposes, and audiences.
	SL.3.1 Engage effectively in a range of collaborative discussions (one-on-one, in groups, and teacher-led) with diverse partners on grade 3 topics and texts, building on others' ideas and expressing their own clearly.
	SL.3.2 Determine the main ideas and supporting details of a text read aloud or information presented in diverse media and formats, including visually, quantitatively, and orally.
	SL.3.3 Ask and answer questions about information from a speaker, offering appropriate elaboration and detail.
	SL.3.6 Speak in complete sentences when appropriate to task and situation in order to provide requested detail or clarification. (See grade 3 Language standards 1 and 3 here for specific expectations.)
	L.3.1 Demonstrate command of the conventions of standard English grammar and usage when writing or speaking.
	L.3.2 Demonstrate command of the conventions of standard English capitalization, punctuation, and spelling when writing.
	L.3.3 Use knowledge of language and its conventions when writing, speaking, reading, or listening.

Lesson	Common Core State Standards
Lesson 3.1, *continued*	L.3.6 Acquire and use accurately grade-appropriate conversational, general academic, and domain-specific words and phrases, including those that signal spatial and temporal relationships (e.g., After dinner that night we went looking for them).
Lesson 3.2	RI.3.1 Ask and answer questions to demonstrate understanding of a text, referring explicitly to the text as the basis for the answers.
	RI.3.2 Determine the main idea of a text; recount the key details and explain how they support the main idea.
	RI.3.3 Describe the relationship between a series of historical events, scientific ideas or concepts, or steps in technical procedures in a text, using language that pertains to time, sequence, and cause/effect.
	RI.3.5 Use text features and search tools (e.g., key words, sidebars, hyperlinks) to locate information relevant to a given topic efficiently.
	RI.3.6 Distinguish their own point of view from that of the author of a text.
	RI.3.7 Use information gained from illustrations (e.g., maps, photographs) and the words in a text to demonstrate understanding of the text (e.g., where, when, why, and how key events occur).
	RI.3.9 Compare and contrast the most important points and key details presented in two texts on the same topic.
	RI.3.10 By the end of the year, read and comprehend informational texts, including history/social studies, science, and technical texts, at the high end of the grades 2–3 text complexity band independently and proficiently.
	RF.3.3 Know and apply grade-level phonics and word analysis skills in decoding words.
	RF.3.4 Read with sufficient accuracy and fluency to support comprehension.
	W.3.1 Write opinion pieces on topics or texts, supporting a point of view with reasons.
	W.3.4 With guidance and support from adults, produce writing in which the development and organization are appropriate to task and purpose.
	W.3.5 With guidance and support from peers and adults, develop and strengthen writing as needed by planning, revising, and editing.

Lesson	Common Core State Standards
Lesson 3.2, *continued*	W.3.6 With guidance and support from adults, use technology to produce and publish writing (using keyboarding skills) as well as to interact and collaborate with others.
	W.3.7 Conduct short research projects that build knowledge about a topic.
	W.3.10 Write routinely over extended time frames (time for research, reflection, and revision) and shorter time frames (a single sitting or a day or two) for a range of discipline-specific tasks, purposes, and audiences.
	SL.3.1 Engage effectively in a range of collaborative discussions (one-on-one, in groups, and teacher-led) with diverse partners on grade 3 topics and texts, building on others' ideas and expressing their own clearly.
	SL.3.2 Determine the main ideas and supporting details of a text read aloud or information presented in diverse media and formats, including visually, quantitatively, and orally.
	SL.3.3 Ask and answer questions about information from a speaker, offering appropriate elaboration and detail.
	SL.3.4 Report on a topic or text, tell a story, or recount an experience with appropriate facts and relevant, descriptive details, speaking clearly at an understandable pace.
	SL.3.6 Speak in complete sentences when appropriate to task and situation in order to provide requested detail or clarification. (See grade 3 Language standards 1 and 3 here for specific expectations.)
	L.3.1 Demonstrate command of the conventions of standard English grammar and usage when writing or speaking.
	L.3.2 Demonstrate command of the conventions of standard English capitalization, punctuation, and spelling when writing.
	L.3.3 Use knowledge of language and its conventions when writing, speaking, reading, or listening.
	L.3.4 Determine or clarify the meaning of unknown and multiple-meaning word and phrases based on grade 3 reading and content, choosing flexibly from a range of strategies.
Lesson 3.3	RI.3.1 Ask and answer questions to demonstrate understanding of a text, referring explicitly to the text as the basis for the answers.
	RI.3.2 Determine the main idea of a text; recount the key details and explain how they support the main idea.
	RI.3.6 Distinguish their own point of view from that of the author of a text.

Lesson	Common Core State Standards
Lesson 3.3, *continued*	W.3.2 Write informative/explanatory texts to examine a topic and convey ideas and information clearly.
	W.3.4 With guidance and support from adults, produce writing in which the development and organization are appropriate to task and purpose.
	W.3.10 Write routinely over extended time frames (time for research, reflection, and revision) and shorter time frames (a single sitting or a day or two) for a range of discipline-specific tasks, purposes, and audiences.
	SL.3.1 Engage effectively in a range of collaborative discussions (one-on-one, in groups, and teacher-led) with diverse partners on grade 3 topics and texts, building on others' ideas and expressing their own clearly.
	SL.3.2 Determine the main ideas and supporting details of a text read aloud or information presented in diverse media and formats, including visually, quantitatively, and orally.
	SL.3.6 Speak in complete sentences when appropriate to task and situation in order to provide requested detail or clarification. (See grade 3 Language standards 1 and 3 here for specific expectations.)
	L.3.1 Demonstrate command of the conventions of standard English grammar and usage when writing or speaking.
	L.3.2 Demonstrate command of the conventions of standard English capitalization, punctuation, and spelling when writing.
	L.3.3 Use knowledge of language and its conventions when writing, speaking, reading, or listening.
	L.3.4 Determine or clarify the meaning of unknown and multiple-meaning word and phrases based on grade 3 reading and content, choosing flexibly from a range of strategies.
Lesson 3.4	RL.3.1 Ask and answer questions to demonstrate understanding of a text, referring explicitly to the text as the basis for the answers.
	RL.3.2 Recount stories, including fables, folktales, and myths from diverse cultures; determine the central message, lesson, or moral and explain how it is conveyed through key details in the text.
	RL.3.3 Describe characters in a story (e.g., their traits, motivations, or feelings) and explain how their actions contribute to the sequence of events.

Lesson	Common Core State Standards
Lesson 3.4, *continued*	W.3.3 Write narratives to develop real or imagined experiences or events using effective technique, descriptive details, and clear event sequences.
	W.3.4 With guidance and support from adults, produce writing in which the development and organization are appropriate to task and purpose.
	W.3.10 Write routinely over extended time frames (time for research, reflection, and revision) and shorter time frames (a single sitting or a day or two) for a range of discipline-specific tasks, purposes, and audiences.
	SL.3.1 Engage effectively in a range of collaborative discussions (one-on-one, in groups, and teacher-led) with diverse partners on grade 3 topics and texts, building on others' ideas and expressing their own clearly.
	SL.3.2 Determine the main ideas and supporting details of a text read aloud or information presented in diverse media and formats, including visually, quantitatively, and orally.
	SL.3.6 Speak in complete sentences when appropriate to task and situation in order to provide requested detail or clarification. (See grade 3 Language standards 1 and 3 here for specific expectations.)
	L.3.1 Demonstrate command of the conventions of standard English grammar and usage when writing or speaking.
	L.3.2 Demonstrate command of the conventions of standard English capitalization, punctuation, and spelling when writing.
	L.3.3 Use knowledge of language and its conventions when writing, speaking, reading, or listening.
	L.3.4 Determine or clarify the meaning of unknown and multiple-meaning word and phrases based on grade 3 reading and content, choosing flexibly from a range of strategies.
	L.3.5 Demonstrate understanding of figurative language, word relationships and nuances in word meanings.
	L.3.6 Acquire and use accurately grade-appropriate conversational, general academic, and domain-specific words and phrases, including those that signal spatial and temporal relationships (e.g., After dinner that night we went looking for them).
Lesson 4.1	RL.3.1 Ask and answer questions to demonstrate understanding of a text, referring explicitly to the text as the basis for the answers.

Lesson	Common Core State Standards
Lesson 4.1, *continued*	RL.3.2 Recount stories, including fables, folktales, and myths from diverse cultures; determine the central message, lesson, or moral and explain how it is conveyed through key details in the text.
	RL.3.3 Describe characters in a story (e.g., their traits, motivations, or feelings) and explain how their actions contribute to the sequence of events.
	RL.3.6 Distinguish their own point of view from that of the narrator or those of the characters.
	W.3.1 Write opinion pieces on topics or texts, supporting a point of view with reasons.
	W.3.10 Write routinely over extended time frames (time for research, reflection, and revision) and shorter time frames (a single sitting or a day or two) for a range of discipline-specific tasks, purposes, and audiences.
	SL.3.1 Engage effectively in a range of collaborative discussions (one-on-one, in groups, and teacher-led) with diverse partners on grade 3 topics and texts, building on others' ideas and expressing their own clearly.
	SL.3.2 Determine the main ideas and supporting details of a text read aloud or information presented in diverse media and formats, including visually, quantitatively, and orally.
	SL.3.6 Speak in complete sentences when appropriate to task and situation in order to provide requested detail or clarification. (See grade 3 Language standards 1 and 3 here for specific expectations.)
	L.3.1 Demonstrate command of the conventions of standard English grammar and usage when writing or speaking.
	L.3.2 Demonstrate command of the conventions of standard English capitalization, punctuation, and spelling when writing.
	L.3.3 Use knowledge of language and its conventions when writing, speaking, reading, or listening.
	L.3.4 Determine or clarify the meaning of unknown and multiple-meaning word and phrases based on grade 3 reading and content, choosing flexibly from a range of strategies.
Lesson 4.2	RL.3.1 Ask and answer questions to demonstrate understanding of a text, referring explicitly to the text as the basis for the answers.

Lesson	Common Core State Standards
Lesson 4.2, *continued*	RL.3.2 Recount stories, including fables, folktales, and myths from diverse cultures; determine the central message, lesson, or moral and explain how it is conveyed through key details in the text.
	RL.3.3 Describe characters in a story (e.g., their traits, motivations, or feelings) and explain how their actions contribute to the sequence of events.
	RL.3.4 Determine the meaning of words and phrases as they are used in a text, distinguishing literal from nonliteral language.
	RL.3.6 Distinguish their own point of view from that of the narrator or those of the characters.
	RL.3.7 Explain how specific aspects of a text's illustrations contribute to what is conveyed by the words in a story (e.g., create mood, emphasize aspects of a character or setting).
	RL.3.10 By the end of the year, read and comprehend literature, including stories, dramas, and poetry, at the high end of the grades 2–3 text complexity band independently and proficiently.
	W.3.3 Write narratives to develop real or imagined experiences or events using effective technique, descriptive details, and clear event sequences.
	W.3.10 Write routinely over extended time frames (time for research, reflection, and revision) and shorter time frames (a single sitting or a day or two) for a range of discipline-specific tasks, purposes, and audiences.
	SL.3.1 Engage effectively in a range of collaborative discussions (one-on-one, in groups, and teacher-led) with diverse partners on grade 3 topics and texts, building on others' ideas and expressing their own clearly.
	SL.3.2 Determine the main ideas and supporting details of a text read aloud or information presented in diverse media and formats, including visually, quantitatively, and orally.
	SL.3.6 Speak in complete sentences when appropriate to task and situation in order to provide requested detail or clarification. (See grade 3 Language standards 1 and 3 here for specific expectations.)
	L.3.1 Demonstrate command of the conventions of standard English grammar and usage when writing or speaking.
	L.3.2 Demonstrate command of the conventions of standard English capitalization, punctuation, and spelling when writing.
	L.3.3 Use knowledge of language and its conventions when writing, speaking, reading, or listening.

Lesson	Common Core State Standards
Lesson 4.2, *continued*	L.3.4 Determine or clarify the meaning of unknown and multiple-meaning word and phrases based on grade 3 reading and content, choosing flexibly from a range of strategies.
Lesson 4.3	RI.3.1 Ask and answer questions to demonstrate understanding of a text, referring explicitly to the text as the basis for the answers.
	RI.3.2 Determine the main idea of a text; recount the key details and explain how they support the main idea.
	RI.3.3 Describe the relationship between a series of historical events, scientific ideas or concepts, or steps in technical procedures in a text, using language that pertains to time, sequence, and cause/effect.
	RI.3.4 Determine the meaning of general academic and domain-specific words and phrases in a text relevant to a grade 3 topic or subject area.
	RI.3.6 Distinguish their own point of view from that of the author of a text.
	RI.3.7 Use information gained from illustrations (e.g., maps, photographs) and the words in a text to demonstrate understanding of the text (e.g., where, when, why, and how key events occur).
	RI.3.10 By the end of the year, read and comprehend informational texts, including history/social studies, science, and technical texts, at the high end of the grades 2–3 text complexity band independently and proficiently.
	W.3.3 Write narratives to develop real or imagined experiences or events using effective technique, descriptive details, and clear event sequences.
	W.3.10 Write routinely over extended time frames (time for research, reflection, and revision) and shorter time frames (a single sitting or a day or two) for a range of discipline-specific tasks, purposes, and audiences.
	SL.3.1 Engage effectively in a range of collaborative discussions (one-on-one, in groups, and teacher-led) with diverse partners on grade 3 topics and texts, building on others' ideas and expressing their own clearly.
	SL.3.2 Determine the main ideas and supporting details of a text read aloud or information presented in diverse media and formats, including visually, quantitatively, and orally.

Lesson	Common Core State Standards
Lesson 4.3, *continued*	SL.3.6 Speak in complete sentences when appropriate to task and situation in order to provide requested detail or clarification. (See grade 3 Language standards 1 and 3 here for specific expectations.)
	L.3.1 Demonstrate command of the conventions of standard English grammar and usage when writing or speaking.
	L.3.2 Demonstrate command of the conventions of standard English capitalization, punctuation, and spelling when writing.
	L.3.3 Use knowledge of language and its conventions when writing, speaking, reading, or listening.
	L.3.4 Determine or clarify the meaning of unknown and multiple-meaning word and phrases based on grade 3 reading and content, choosing flexibly from a range of strategies.
Lesson 4.4	RI.3.1 Ask and answer questions to demonstrate understanding of a text, referring explicitly to the text as the basis for the answers.
	RI.3.4 Determine the meaning of general academic and domain-specific words and phrases in a text relevant to a grade 3 topic or subject area.
	RI.3.5 Use text features and search tools (e.g., key words, sidebars, hyperlinks) to locate information relevant to a given topic efficiently.
	RI.3.6 Distinguish their own point of view from that of the author of a text.
	RI.3.9 Compare and contrast the most important points and key details presented in two texts on the same topic.
	RI.3.10 By the end of the year, read and comprehend informational texts, including history/social studies, science, and technical texts, at the high end of the grades 2–3 text complexity band independently and proficiently.
	W.3.2 Write informative/explanatory texts to examine a topic and convey ideas and information clearly.
	W.3.10 Write routinely over extended time frames (time for research, reflection, and revision) and shorter time frames (a single sitting or a day or two) for a range of discipline-specific tasks, purposes, and audiences.
	SL.3.1 Engage effectively in a range of collaborative discussions (one-on-one, in groups, and teacher-led) with diverse partners on grade 3 topics and texts, building on others' ideas and expressing their own clearly.

Lesson	Common Core State Standards
Lesson 4.4, *continued*	SL.3.2 Determine the main ideas and supporting details of a text read aloud or information presented in diverse media and formats, including visually, quantitatively, and orally.
	SL.3.6 Speak in complete sentences when appropriate to task and situation in order to provide requested detail or clarification. (See grade 3 Language standards 1 and 3 here for specific expectations.)
	L.3.1 Demonstrate command of the conventions of standard English grammar and usage when writing or speaking.
	L.3.2 Demonstrate command of the conventions of standard English capitalization, punctuation, and spelling when writing.
	L.3.3 Use knowledge of language and its conventions when writing, speaking, reading, or listening.
Lesson 4.5	RL.3.1 Ask and answer questions to demonstrate understanding of a text, referring explicitly to the text as the basis for the answers.
	RL.3.2 Recount stories, including fables, folktales, and myths from diverse cultures; determine the central message, lesson, or moral and explain how it is conveyed through key details in the text.
	RL.3.3 Describe characters in a story (e.g., their traits, motivations, or feelings) and explain how their actions contribute to the sequence of events.
	RL.3.4 Determine the meaning of words and phrases as they are used in a text, distinguishing literal from nonliteral language.
	RL.3.5 Refer to parts of stories, dramas, and poems when writing or speaking about a text, using terms such as chapter, scene, and stanza; describe how each successive part builds on earlier sections.
	RL.3.6 Distinguish their own point of view from that of the narrator or those of the characters.
	RL.3.10 By the end of the year, read and comprehend literature, including stories, dramas, and poetry, at the high end of the grades 2–3 text complexity band independently and proficiently.
	RF.3.4 Read with sufficient accuracy and fluency to support comprehension.
	W.3.3 Write narratives to develop real or imagined experiences or events using effective technique, descriptive details, and clear event sequences.

Lesson	Common Core State Standards
Lesson 4.5, *continued*	W.3.4 With guidance and support from adults, produce writing in which the development and organization are appropriate to task and purpose.
	W.3.5 With guidance and support from peers and adults, develop and strengthen writing as needed by planning, revising, and editing.
	W.3.6 With guidance and support from adults, use technology to produce and publish writing (using keyboarding skills) as well as to interact and collaborate with others.
	W.3.10 Write routinely over extended time frames (time for research, reflection, and revision) and shorter time frames (a single sitting or a day or two) for a range of discipline-specific tasks, purposes, and audiences.
	SL.3.1 Engage effectively in a range of collaborative discussions (one-on-one, in groups, and teacher-led) with diverse partners on grade 3 topics and texts, building on others' ideas and expressing their own clearly.
	SL.3.2 Determine the main ideas and supporting details of a text read aloud or information presented in diverse media and formats, including visually, quantitatively, and orally.
	SL.3.6 Speak in complete sentences when appropriate to task and situation in order to provide requested detail or clarification. (See grade 3 Language standards 1 and 3 here for specific expectations.)
	L.3.1 Demonstrate command of the conventions of standard English grammar and usage when writing or speaking.
	L.3.2 Demonstrate command of the conventions of standard English capitalization, punctuation, and spelling when writing.
	L.3.3 Use knowledge of language and its conventions when writing, speaking, reading, or listening.
	L.3.4 Determine or clarify the meaning of unknown and multiple-meaning word and phrases based on grade 3 reading and content, choosing flexibly from a range of strategies.
	L.3.5 Demonstrate understanding of figurative language, word relationships and nuances in word meanings.
	L.3.6 Acquire and use accurately grade-appropriate conversational, general academic, and domain-specific words and phrases, including those that signal spatial and temporal relationships (e.g., After dinner that night we went looking for them).